HEBREWS

THROUGH A

HEBREW'S

EYES

HEBREWS

THROUGH A

HEBREW'S

EYES

HOPE IN THE MIDST
OF A HOPELESS WORLD

DR. STUART SACKS

Messianic Jewish Publishers
a division of
Lederer/Messianic Jewish Communications
Baltimore, Maryland

DEDICATED TO RAY DILLARD

Who is sure of what we hope for and
certain of what we do not see.

Published 1995
Printed in the United States of America
Cover design by Now You See it! graphics

04 03 02 01 00 99   6 5 4 3 2 1

ISBN 1-880226-61-8

Messianic Jewish Publishers
a division of
Lederer/Messianic Jewish Communications
6204 Park Heights Avenue
Baltimore, Maryland 21215
(410) 358-6471

Distributed by
Lederer/Messianic Jewish Resources International
order line: (800) 410-7367
e-mail: lederer@messianicjewish.net
Internet: http://www.MessianicJewish.net

CONTENTS

PREFACE

This book has been written to provide a unique understanding of a letter originally written to encourage and sustain a small group of Jewish believers living nearly 2,000 years ago. I have used my own Jewish heritage as a backdrop for examining some of the major elements of the Letter to the Hebrews.

Since the first century when the letter was written, Orthodox Jewish thinking has remained essentially unchanged. I have drawn on my personal knowledge of that perspective to give the reader a Semitic perspective on the contents of the letter and the outlook of those who first read it.

I have chosen not to comment on every verse in the Letter to the Hebrews; rather, I've addressed those portions that my Orthodox education and upbringing shed light on to help you better understand this encouraging book of the Bible.

If you see a reference to a portion of Scripture that does not identify a book, like (4:20), it comes from the book of Hebrews. Other references are identified.

May God use my book to bring more hope into your life.

INTRODUCTION

The original community to whom the Letter to the Hebrews was sent probably lived in Asia Minor (known today as Turkey) before the destruction of the Temple in 70 C.E. (The term C.E., or Common Era, is used in this text in place of the usual term A.D. to indicate the time since the coming of Messiah. The term B.C.E. refers to the period Before the Common Era.) These new followers of the Messiah were experiencing stressful times. The possibility that some of them might lapse back into a Judaism without the Messiah was doubtless never far from the author's thinking.

No one knows for certain who wrote Hebrews. We are probably well advised simply to echo the words of Origen (3rd Century): "God alone knows."

This epistle is every bit as much a sermon as it is a letter. The writer may have intended it to serve as a document to be circulated for the edification of many congregations of believers. History has surely proved that to be what happened.

Hebrews' solid doctrinal elements spill over into everyday life. Hebrews alone in the New Testament actually calls Yeshua (Jesus) our priest. His priesthood is a permanent reality with direct consequences for all who trust in him. The writer refers to the Messiah as *kohen gadol* (4:14). It was his way of saying that Yeshua was (and is) a "great High Priest."

Having our High Priest in heaven has a direct bearing on everything we do. Because he always lives to intercede for us, we can have confidence that nothing can ultimately wrench us from God's loving care. We often find ourselves in a wilderness overrun with hazards which threaten to overwhelm us. It is then that we must remember both the greatness and the work of him who has saved us.

In times of strife, especially, we need to know and be strengthened by the fact that Yeshua, our High Priest, is faithfully praying for us. We need his death. We need his resurrection. We need his intercession. We need him in his divine glory and in his manhood.

All that we need God has promised to provide. For that reason, we can "hold on to our courage" (3:6) and "stand fast until the end" (3:14), "taking hold of the hope offered us" (6:18).

I am not usually partial to being exhorted unless, of course, something extremely urgent needs to be addressed. If my well-being, present or future, is on the line, it's a good thing to be prodded in the right direction.

I recall the exhortations of my rabbi to obey the *Torah* (Law). I wasn't singled out for this; all my people were subject to the demands of the *Torah*. From childhood, traditional Jewish education revolves around the daily study of the *Torah*, the five books of Moses.

For the more orthodox, that study also involved reading the works of revered Jewish scholars, as in the *Talmud*, the codified body of Jewish law, and commentators such as the medieval scholar, Rashi. We heard the Law read and chanted regularly in the synagogue on *Shabbat* (Sabbath); to disregard its dictates was to court disaster.

The recipients of the New Testament document called Hebrews (a title not in the original manuscript) were also being urged to listen patiently to an extended exhortation. Owing to the magnitude of its theme, the author actually considered his thirteen chapters of material to be "brief" (13:22).

He is writing to a people under siege, Jewish believers who are in need of encouragement. It is as if they were in the midst of a wilderness experience every bit as intense as the desert wanderings of their ancestors.

These people could cry out with the desperate words of David which launch Psalm 69: *Ba-u mayim ad nefesh,* "The waters have risen up to my soul."

An overtly hostile environment threatened to destroy their precious seedling faith in a crucified, yet risen, Messiah. The forces arrayed against them were formidable, yet not all physical.

From within their hearts, the old ways of seeking to *earn* God's acceptance by Law and Temple ritual beckoned them. Perhaps it would be proper, after all, to return to those fundamentals and squarely place their faith in the long-accepted, God-ordained traditions. But to do so would necessitate a return to pursuits which had utterly failed to bring peace to their society or to their souls.

At the heart of my people's hope has been the coming of *ha-Mashiakh,* the Messiah. Israel's national anthem, *Hatikvah* (The Hope), expresses a longing for a freedom which cannot be separated from the Messiah. The Jewish scholar Maimonides spoke for the nation when he said, "All the prophets have established the fact that the Messiah will redeem Israel." And he will be, Israel believes, a direct descendant of David *ha-melekh* (the king), who will come to liberate them finally from all oppression and establish his eternal, benevolent reign.

The Lubavitch Hasidim have been a powerful and vastly influential Jewish sect for many years. Their leader, the late Menachem Mendel Schneerson, was called the *Rebbe.* The title denotes more than an ordinary rabbi. His tremendous wisdom and influence led many to believe that he was the Messiah. Some of his followers believe that God may actually raise him from the dead in confirmation of his messiahship.

In Jewish thought, the advent of the Messiah will occur *b'akherit ha-yamim,* (in the latter end of the days.) That is the expression employed by the writer of Hebrews in his opening words to bolster the spirits of the believers who were under fire. Since the basis of their hope was to be found in him, the author took great pains to establish the greatness of the Messiah's person and the immensity of his accomplishments for all those who by faith embraced him as their Lord and savior.

Martin Buber, the Jewish philosopher, once equated religious experience with the exceptional, with the ecstatic. Later, he came to accept his ordinary moment-by-moment encounters with others as the very heart of everything that was spiritually genuine. Unlike this Jewish sage, the writer of Hebrews believes in a God who may be personally known, with whom one may actually speak and upon whom one may totally rely.

Although such contact does not relieve a believer of daily obligations or lift him out of life's struggles, God becomes for that person a transcendent reality, a dynamic personal power rather than an ethical ideal or a philosophical abstraction. The needy believer is free, even invited, to approach God confidently in order to receive his mercy and grace. For this reason, the author of Hebrews knows it is possible to hold fast to the confession of faith that links him to the Messiah.

Hebrews speaks to the deepest needs of the hearts of all who find themselves in the wilderness. In a crisis situation, it is common to hear one Jewish person challenge another to have *bitakhon* (trust in God). God speaks through this Hebrew writer of a number of Jewish heroes who demonstrated that trust even in the hardest times.

Most importantly, God speaks to his children through the one identified by the prophets as *Mashiakh*, that is, Messiah, the Anointed One. This deliverer is a very present help in trouble and the guarantor of eternal blessings. So let us, as the author exhorts, "fix our eyes on Yeshua" (12:2).

Although we do not know for certain who wrote Hebrews, we do know that the author intended to exhort God's people through many warnings and admonitions (13:22). No higher view of the Messiah is to be found anywhere in Scripture (1:3), nor is there a more compelling explanation concerning the finality of his high priestly sacrifice (chapters 9–10). But these great theological teachings are intended to serve as the basis for action.

The fact that we now have a better covenant ("better" occurs thirteen times in the letter) should stimulate us to be on guard against

indifference lest we drift away from the truth; we must give "more
earnest heed to the things we have heard" (2:1). Sin is terribly deceitful
(3:13); we must therefore be diligent in appropriating the means of
grace. The warnings about defection are real warnings; but his means of
effectively sustaining us until the end are equally real. "Let us therefore
come boldly to the throne of grace, that we may obtain mercy and find
grace to help in time of need" (4:16).

Hebrews leads to the resources that are available when life threatens
to overwhelm us. Here we can find the strength to resolve and overcome life's relentless pressures.

CHAPTER ONE

HE HAS SPOKEN TO US BY HIS SON
HEBREWS 1:2

HEBREWS 1

Two decades ago, Alex Haley's best-selling book, *Roots*, helped fuel the black pride movement as African-Americans began to reflect on the significance of their ancestry. For Jewish people, history has always been ✓ a vital part of our orientation towards life.

In Jewish thought, the greatest of the patriarchs is *Avraham avinu* ○ (Abraham our father). Abraham, his son Isaac and grandson Jacob are • called *ha-avot* (the fathers). We look to these figures for personal and spiritual identity.

At the celebration of Passover, it is incumbent upon every Jew to ✓ consciously identify with his ancestors who were, by God's grace, liberated from the land of Egypt, out of the house of bondage. There is time set aside to reflect on this. *Shemot* (the Book of Exodus) is traditionally read in the synagogue during the weeks preceding Passover.

In the fall, the festival of *Sukkot* (Booths) reminds us of our desert • wanderings following the escape from Egypt. For an entire week, especially in Israel, small hut-like dwellings become temporary residences blanketing the landscape in celebration of God's presence with us ○ throughout our lengthy trek to the land of promise.

Yet it is not these festivals alone which call the Jew to remember *Yetsiat Mitzrayim* (the exodus from Egypt); every prayer, every religious event, compels us to recall our history's chief frame of reference; even the songs of *Hanukkah* celebrate the Passover's central historical significance.

Will Herberg, the influential twentieth-century scholar of Judaic studies and philosophy, called Exodus-Sinai "the interpretive center of redemptive history." Our history supplies our identity.

We are fortunate that our ancestors spoke with authority and clarity about life's most important matters. Some of these people were set apart by God and called *nevi'im* (prophets). These prominent figures not only told us what God expected of us, but also strengthened us through telling our people what we could expect of him.

Hebrews 1:1 insists that "God spoke to our forefathers through [literally, 'in'] the prophets." Although the means of divine communication were never made clear, it is worth noting that the titles of the Old Testament books were given with full consideration of the gravity of that communication.

For example, *Devarim* (Deuteronomy) takes its title from the opening phrase, *Eleh ha-devarim*, "These are the words." Moses' teaching began with the declaration, "The Lord our God said to us" (Deuteronomy 1:6). The book we refer to by its Latin derivative, Leviticus, is called in Hebrew, *Vayikra*. This is taken from its first words, "And he called."

Learning the words of God is critical. That's why study is so highly regarded in the Jewish community. *Yeshivot* (seminaries) are deemed vitally necessary for Jewish boys who want to understand the fullness of their heritage. There are even seminaries for married men whose full-time devotion to Hebrew thought requires hours of study each day.

According to the *Talmud,* God will one day ask every Jew if he was diligent in setting aside a regular time for study. Israel's hope, it is reasoned, cannot survive if it is detached from that which God has communicated to her.

The writer of Hebrews knew that only an intensified personal understanding of God's final and decisive communication would generate the resilient, sustaining faith they so desperately needed.

The first readers of Hebrews were part of a community whose recent history and experiences had been tragically discouraging. Following Israel's captivity in Babylon, hopes were revived for the return of the visible manifestation of God. Yet the prophecies of Haggai and Zechariah regarding the return of God's *sh'khinah*, his dwelling glory, to a rebuilt Temple had not been realized. Five centuries of frustration followed.

In the generation preceding Yeshua's time, revolts and other bloodshed took the lives of more than 100,000 Jews. In 31 B.C.E., an earthquake had killed another 30,000. Severe famine and pestilence also took their toll. Herod (so-called "the Great") bled the land mercilessly with unrelenting taxation, a blight which continued long after his death. Messages of hope were rarely heard; despair was everywhere. The average person felt the bleakness of the times and longed for relief, something to buoy his spirits.

In this depressing situation, the writer of Hebrews urged his readers to look at Messiah quite differently from the usual way, as the coming liberator.

The most prominent Jewish expectation associated with Messiah was the exaltation of the Davidic throne. This would be accompanied by a golden age of peace and joy. No rabbi anticipated the magnitude of his glory as it is capsulized here in the opening sentence of Hebrews (1:1–4).

The commonly held Jewish views of Messiah required radical revision. He is no mere monarch, not even a super-David, but a being of awe-inspiring nature. God had identified with man by becoming a man. In him and through him, God had spoken most conclusively and completely. Nothing remained to be said, for "The Son is the radiance of God's glory and the exact representation of his being" (1:3).

When Jewish people speak of the glory of God they use the word *kavod*. The word conveys the idea of "heaviness." In our age, concepts

9

of God are characterized by a kind of weightlessness. You hear it in the songs, the prayers, the attitudes of people. But for Israel, God's "weightiness" is seen in all that he is and all that he does.

The glory that Israel witnessed on Sinai (Exodus 24:16) also filled all of God's world (Isaiah 6:3). Now that same *kavod*, revealed in his Messiah, the Son, could be known by all who trusted in his saving work. The writer of Hebrews wanted to strengthen the followers of Yeshua by helping them focus on the greatness of their Lord and savior.

What was true for first century believers is equally true today. We must, in facing life's hardships, develop an abiding preoccupation with our glorious Lord. John Owen, the prominent seventeenth century Puritan, emphasized the point by saying, "If I have observed anything by experience it is this: a man may take the measure of his growth and decay in grace according to his thoughts and meditations upon the person of Christ, and the glory of Christ."

Jeremiah's Book of Lamentations is called in Hebrew, *Eykha*, based on its first word, "How," which becomes a mournful sigh when spoken. The book is read each year, traditionally by candlelight, sitting on the ground in an atmosphere of gloom; it is often chanted to a sad melody.

While its contents point to the destruction of Jerusalem and Solomon's Temple, its annual reading is also the occasion for remembering other painful events, such as the razing of the Second Temple in 70 C.E. and the Jewish expulsion from Spain in 1492.

All this collective sadness leads the Jewish people to poignantly recall that they have certainly not been the masters of their fate. This led to the writing of many prayers acknowledging that everything happens at the Lord's command. One such prayer, *Aleynu*, begins by confessing that "it is our duty (*aleynu*) to praise the master of all," to proclaim the greatness of him who shaped all things. The prayer acknowledges the blessed Holy One of Israel to be "the supreme king of kings."

Hebrews 1:3 reveals that "after [the Messiah] had provided purification for sins, he sat down at the right hand of the majesty on high." On the same theme, verse 8 continues, "Your throne, O God, will last forever and ever..." Hebrews goes further, however, and confronts us

10

with a cosmic person who must be greater than even our most imaginative conception of him. He is "the exact representation" of God. Not only has he come to us in our need, he is also actively "sustaining all things by his powerful word" (1:3). The universe is nothing less than the handiwork of the Messiah (1:2).

No dry doctrine this! It is impossible to estimate the importance of this truth to the Hebrew believers. Branded *meshumadim* (traitors to Israel's faith), the rejection by family and friends needed to be offset by the love and full acceptance they received from God's eternal Messiah, the God-Man, sustainer of all things.

I recall, more than half a life-time ago, when I confessed my belief in Yeshua before the disgruntled rabbi in whose synagogue I had received my spiritual education. "How," he asked, "can you identify yourself with those who have persecuted us?"

Although I was young in the faith, I knew enough to tell the rabbi that a true follower of the Messiah, whether or not he called himself a "Christian," would never harm another person, regardless of his ethnic roots. In desperation my rabbi suggested that I was *meshugah* (crazy) and gave me the name of a Jewish psychiatrist.

During the long ride home from the synagogue, I recall being filled with sorrow. I knew that none of my family relationships could be untouched by what had happened. I sensed I was entering my own *midbar* (wilderness) and wondered how I'd survive.

But the Messiah had become real to me through the words his disciples had written. Following him was not simply an option. There was for me, as a popular Hebrew saying goes, *eyn b'rera* (no alternative). One cannot easily dismiss him who created all things and holds them all together (Colossians 1:16–17).

It was not that I was cleaving to him; he was holding me together and pressing me to himself. The psalmist's words expressed my reality: "You hem me in behind and before; you have laid your hand upon me" (Psalm 139:5).

Rabbi Chaim ben Attar observed that Abraham himself was a convert. What matters is not that one is converted, but what one is converted to.

11

In one of the *midrashim* (Bible commentaries) it is said that "the converted [to Judaism] are beloved to God." But for me and the Jews reading Hebrews, the experience of God's love could no longer be sought or contained within perfunctory Jewish observance. We found our heritage fulfilled in a person, God's Messiah.

Some speak disparagingly of our *giyur* (conversion), but we could more appropriately call this step "completion" or, to borrow a Messianic term, *ge'ulah*, redemption.

CHAPTER TWO

BRINGING MANY SONS TO GLORY
HEBREWS 2:10

HEBREWS 2:1–13

In order to understand the deeply felt Jewish expectations which preceded the coming of *Yeshua ha-Notzri* (Jesus the Nazarene), we can consider a collection of hymns that date back to the Roman occupation of Judea. The Psalms of Solomon were written just prior to the coming of Messiah. They speak with yearning anticipation of God's intervention, his messianic salvation. Most likely written by Pharisees, none expresses the Israeli's national hope more vividly than the seventeenth:

> *See, Lord; raise up for them their king, the son of David,*
> *In a time which thou knowest, O God, that he may reign over*
> *Israel thy servant,*
> *And gird him with strength to dash in pieces the unjust rulers...*
> *He will possess the nations, to serve him under his yoke,*
> *And he will glorify the Lord with the praise of all the earth.*
> *He will cleanse Jerusalem in holiness, as it was from the beginning,*
> *That the nations may come from the ends of the earth to see his*
> *glory,*

Bearing gifts for her sons that were utterly weakened,
And to see the glory of the Lord wherewith God has glorified her.
A righteous king, one taught by God, is he who rules over them,
And there will be no unrighteousness among them all his days,
For all will be holy, and their king is the Lord Messiah.

Several themes dominate the hymn, not the least of which are those revealing the worshipper's desire for cleansing, holiness and righteousness. The experience of glory is bound up with personal purity for "God is good to those who are pure in heart" (Psalm 73:1).

The writer to the Hebrews focuses on these quintessential qualities. The Lord will bring his many sons and daughters to glory and the route to that final, blessed state will be through the work of God alone.

Jews in every age have lived with a paradox with respect to being pure before God. On one hand, great emphasis is placed on striving to obey the Law. On the other, purification is something which the Lord alone can accomplish. Although impossible to achieve, there is a dogged determination toward purity among religious Jews.

One doesn't have to look long into the *Tenakh* (Old Testament) to realize the significance of the Law. Its demands became the pivotal point for all who desired purity.

This orientation can, in part, be traced to Israel's history following her repatriation from Babylon in the sixth century B.C.E. In the absence of any revived Davidic dynasty, synagogues developed, and the emphasis turned from the ritual of the Temple to a deepening attention to the Law. With the study of the Law came the burgeoning system of demands.

The *Talmud* noted that 613 *mitzvot* (commandments) are found in the *Torah*. The Hebrew word *mitzvah*, singular for *mitzvot*, also means good deed. So, for many Jews, myself as a boy included, the performance of the *mitzvot* would hopefully commend us to God. "Visit your sick aunt, Stuart; do a *mitzvah*!" was an exhortation which would prick and inspire my conscience's quest for righteousness.

14

Following the first century C.E. an expanded *Talmudic* legal code developed that became extraordinarily complex, requiring rabbinic experts for interpretation. It was easy to lose oneself in the study of the Law, its precepts and applications, to attempt to fulfill one's vision of the Almighty's plan.

The *Talmud* states that the world stands upon three things: *Torah* study, worship, and *gemilut chasadim* (good deeds). The rabbi's primary responsibility then, as now, is not the preaching of sermons or visiting the sick; it is interpreting the demands of the Law. This is no secondary emphasis in the religious leader's ministry, for the great Rabbi Hillel, an older contemporary of Yeshua, said, "Who has gained for himself words of *Torah* has gained for himself the life of the world to come."

At a meeting of Jewish and Christian theologians in New York City, an orthodox rabbi expressed the tension of this approach to life by saying, "In the final analysis, I know I cannot perfectly obey the Law in its entirety; I must rely on the mercy of God. Yet I cannot with absolute certainty know that God will be merciful."

Against the uncertainty spawned by a religious system whose basic approach to life could be summed up, "Do this!" the Letter to the Hebrews says, "Trust him!"

According to the rabbis, the world might stand on study, worship and good deeds. But first century believers, like twentieth century believers, stood on the fact that Yeshua the Messiah fulfilled the Law's demands on their behalf. He "provided purification for sins" (1:3). The Holy Savior "suffered death" for them (2:9). The grace by which Messiah accepts the full penalty of sin as our substitute should lead us to understand our relationship to him as one between "brothers" (2:11), adopted members of God's very own family!

The Pharisees extended hope only to those who, according to another of the Psalms of Solomon, could "walk in the righteousness of [God's] commandments." The Gospel extends its unique hope to all those whose walk, whose way of life, was singularly bound up with the Messiah's free gift of righteousness.

15

Our confidence, even our boast, is in the perfection of another, in him "who makes men holy," making us children in the family of God and infinitely precious to him (2:11).

The little flock of believers needed to hear, not only of God's provision for them in heaven, but also of his help for them on earth. They needed to know that what God had done for them in his son is not reserved solely for what Israel called *ha-olam ha-ba*, the next world.

Jews always believed in the necessity of making the most out of their lives in *ha-olam ha-zeh*, this world. Thus the Hebrews were told that Messiah suffered being mindful of his people's needs during times of personal crisis (2:18), and that he is able to sympathize with them in their weakness (4:15).

These Jewish believers understood what it meant to hope in the Lord with passionate and emotional conviction. During Yeshua's time, legalism had not yet taken such a strong hold on the Jewish religious mind. The people of ancient Israel showed a passionate faith in God that is rarely displayed, today. Their hopeful fervor is captured in a famous ancient festival which Yeshua attended.

The last day of the feast that commemorates the wilderness wanderings (*Sukkot*) was called *Hoshanah Rabbah* (literally, "the great 'Save, we plead!'"). Prayers were offered up, wave upon wave, for protection from everything from oppression to miscarriage. Particularly, prayers were made for sufficient rainfall to support the crops necessary for survival.

In Yeshua's day, a priest of Israel daily fetched water from Jerusalem's Pool of Siloam and carried it to the Temple where it would be poured out against the altar as a libation before the Lord. Yet the water ritual was not conducted on the final day, the day of *Hoshanah Rabbah*.

John tells us, on "the last and greatest day of the feast, Yeshua stood and said in a loud voice, 'If anyone is thirsty let him come to me and drink. Whoever believes in me, as the Scripture has said, streams of living water will flow from within him'" (John 7:37–38). It's a fantastic statement, one that the Messiah had earlier personalized for the benefit of a Samaritan woman: "...whoever drinks the water I give him will never thirst. Indeed, the water I give him will become in him a spring welling up to eternal life" (John 4:14).

Centuries earlier the greatest of the Messianic prophets spoke of him who would become Israel's salvation: "*Yah, YHVH* [the name of God] has become my strength and my song; he also is become my salvation; and with joy shall you draw water out of the wells of salvation" (Isaiah 12:2–3).

The Hebrew root, *yasha*, which translates into words like "save" and "salvation" also gives us *Yeshua*, or Jesus. I like to envision some early Jewish believer reading Isaiah 12, rejoicing as he says that the God of his salvation has now become "my Yeshua."

The Psalms of Solomon observed man's state as "utterly weakened" and cried out for one who was without weakness. Yet the Messiah's perfection was achieved through his suffering.

First, he had to be tested, tempted in every way so that he could offer himself as a Paschal lamb without spot or blemish (4:15). The perfect deliverer would also have to endure suffering unto death in order to free his people from death's dreadful tyranny (2:9, 14–15). Finally, he personally would have to endure suffering in order to empathize fully with and assist those who were confronting severe trials (2:18).

For the sufferer, there's something remarkably comforting in the knowledge that God, himself, knows what it is to suffer, that he has not exempted himself from the traumas of human life.

When the Jew was carried off to ancient Babylon, he used an Aramaic expression which became an instant part of his speech: *rachmana litslan!* ("God forbid!"). Then, as now, its hopeful cry confronts hostility and pain.

At the festival of Purim (the holiday based on the Book of Esther), the children sing a song remembering Israel's deliverance from the wicked Persian, Haman. One of the verses says, "You got a pain? Crunch it underfoot. Open your mouth and sing; let's all joke and drink; let's live, despite all our troubles..." But not all of life's problems can be met with that kind of bravura. Even if our existence is relatively pleasant, we all must ultimately face the fear of death.

Concerning the fear of death, the Letter to the Hebrews offers much to console us. Not the least of its comfort comes from the message that glory, not the grave, is our final destiny. Our passageway has been cleared of all obstacles by him who became our perfect savior through suffering. In his oneness with us, we can rest assured that Yeshua is not ashamed of us (2:11).

Three Old Testament texts are cited to give added depth to that statement. They are not isolated proof-texts, but include the context of their original setting. The first is from Psalm 22. After intense suffering, the psalmist joyfully proclaims, even sings, the name of his father to all his children (verse 22). It is a foreshadowing of the triumph following the Messiah's intense ordeal.

We recall the piercing of our savior's hands and feet, his cry of agony, his acute awareness of the dreaded separation from his father, the cruel mockery of his accusers, and the casting of lots for his garments. All were foretold prophetically, centuries before by the psalmist. The remarkable text once again reminds the Hebrews of the depth of his savior's love, a love that will surely not abandon him in times of trouble.

The writer then brings forward the testimony of Isaiah in two parts. "I will put my trust in him" (Isaiah 8:17) is accompanied by the prophet's determination to "wait for the Lord who is hiding his face from the house of Jacob." Surely, the Hebrew believers felt desolate. Like so many who had accepted Yeshua as the Messiah, they had been cut off from family and friends. They wondered why the Lord had not revealed himself to them, also. This is a question that I—and most Jewish believers— still ask. Yet the mystery of his sovereign, electing love is unfathomable.

Isaiah knew that his own message would fall on deaf ears (Isaiah 6:10; 53:1), but that it was all part of God's inscrutable plan. In desolate moments we, like the prophets of old, are still called to trust him who always "works for the good of those who love him" (Romans 8:28).

Hebrews' final reference (2:13) quotes Isaiah again: "Here am I and the children God has given me" (Isaiah 8:18). Here, too, the Savior speaks with his prophet's words, telling us that we are truly members of his family. God has, in the words of Isaiah, set us forth as "signs" and "symbols" (Isaiah 8:18). Each believer is the miraculous result of God's intervention in his or her life, a sign that points heavenward to the incomparable wonder of his irresistible grace. That grace will never fail the believer, for his destiny has been established by him who prayed, "Father, I want those you have given me to be with me where I am, and to see my glory" (John 17:24).

CHAPTER THREE

FIX YOUR EYES ON YESHUA
HEBREWS 3:1

HEBREWS 2:14–3:1

In the little book called *Kohelet* (Ecclesiastes), King Solomon observed that although God has set eternity in the hearts of men, the topic is an enigma (Ecclesiastes 3:11–12). The frustration he felt was expressed in the well-known words of *Kohelet*, "all is meaningless."

The book is traditionally read during *Sukkot,* the festival commemorating the wilderness wanderings. At the end of the book, the teacher declares, "God will bring every deed into judgment, including every hidden thing" (Ecclesiastes 12:14). But, there is no comfort in the critical assessment of our deeds. None of us can stand before God unashamed.

Jewish orthodoxy has held tenaciously to the prospect of an afterlife. Yet even the godly of Hebrew history have failed to grasp its reality. Hezekiah, one of Judah's spiritually vital kings, became ill to the point of death and "wept bitterly" (Isaiah 38:3). He said, "In the prime of life must I go through the gates of death and be robbed of the rest of my years?…I will not again see the LORD, the LORD, in the land of the living..." (Isaiah 38:10–11). Even David sang dolefully, "No one remembers you when he is dead. Who praises you from the grave?" (Psalm 6:5).

Despite these protests, Jewish hope faithfully acknowledges a *tekhiyat ha metim* (resurrection of the dead). At the end of time the righteous are expected to come back to life in this world.

One of the oldest customs of Israel, performed in anticipation of the resurrection, involves the washing of the dead body, trimming and combing the hair, and wrapping the corpse in white linen. This cleansing ritual is known as *taharah* (purification). It is often performed by a select volunteer organization known as *khevrah kadishah*, a "holy society." Usually a man will be wrapped in his prayer shawl. It is more important than a coffin which, in Israel, is customarily made of crude, unpolished wood. After the dead have been prepared, they are accompanied to the burial site where mourners will each take a turn shoveling earth into the grave. Those closest to the deceased customarily rend their garments in the tradition of the grief-stricken, from the collar downward.

At my father's grave I recall saying the ancient prayer called *kaddish* (sanctification) along with the small company of mourners. Yet as we solemnly intoned the words, there was no voice of comfort. The darkened skies, the hush of nature, all seemed to conspire against hope.

The opening words of that ancient Hebrew prayer which we spoke hopefully to one another as well as to God were, "May he establish his kingdom in your lifetime, in your days..." Tradition called me to recite the mourner's *kaddish* for many months following my father's death.

Hebrews does not bypass the cemetery but gives assurance that it's not the ultimate destiny of believers.

First the writer states that "Yeshua suffered death so that by the grace of God he might taste death for everyone" (2:9). He has endured the bitterness of death as a pioneer, leading his trusting followers to heaven's splendor. Through the experience of suffering and death Yeshua, the author of salvation, became the perfect Savior (2:10).

Death's awesome power is sin, revealed by the Law's searching judgments. Few things grip a person as tenaciously as the lifelong fear of death (2:15). The *Talmud* says, "The righteous are greater in their death than in their life," but only one righteous man in all history

22

opened the way to eternal greatness for those who entrust themselves to his keeping.

✳ Yeshua vanquished death and drank its bitter dregs in our place. He
• rejoices to consider believers his family (2:11), those who are called in
Hebrew, *mishpakhah*.

The Son of God has gone to prepare a place for his followers and
has promised to return that he might accompany them to their new
home (John 14:2–3). With that prospect before them, the Jewish be- •
lievers could withstand the threats from the surrounding community
and not shrink back from allegiance to the Messiah.

• The writer also discusses the devil's defeat and his lack of power
over believers (2:14). Jewish theologians often place a definite   ar-
ticle before the devil's name, identifying him as *ha-Satan*. The Hebrew
word means "adversary" or "accuser" and is treated by many as a com- •
mon noun rather than as the specific title of a personal, malevolent
being.

Some think of him as a projection of our evil tendencies, or perhaps an angel sent to test the chosen people. It is more consistent with
Scripture to recognize demonic powers as formidable agents of Satan
against whom no human is an even match.

Abba Binyamin, a *Talmudic* writer, said, "If we could view the
mazikim (demons) with our own eyes, there is none among us that
could face them." Although Satan is seldom mentioned in the *Tenakh*, •
we are engaged in an unrelenting spiritual battle against him and his
unseen dark forces (Ephesians 6:12).

Informed Jews of Yeshua's day would have had alternative ways of
referring to him. From the Dead Sea Scrolls we learn that the Qumran •
community called him *Belial* who, along with his minions, sought to
attack the righteous. The ancient scrolls claim that one called the Prince •
of Light would ultimately triumph against him. Strange sounding names •
such as *Mastema* and *Sammael* were also used by Jews to refer to the
evil one.

, Yeshua's enemies attacked him by calling him *Ba'al-zibbul* (possibly
meaning "lord of dung"). Yeshua's response was, "If the Master of the

house has been called *Ba'al-zibbul*, how much more will they speak ill √ of the members of his household!" (Matthew 10:25).

Yeshua took over Satan's household and robbed him of his possessions (see Matthew 12:29). Whether we are Jewish or non-Jewish believers in the Messiah, we were enslaved by the strongest of enemies, but have now been released from that terrible bondage.

Yeshua rightly claimed lordship over his house (3:6) for which he paid the price of his own blood and announced a sweeping victory on our behalf: "If it is by the Spirit of God that I cast out demons, then the √ kingdom of God has come upon you" (Matthew 12:28). In this way he has rendered inestimable help to Abraham's descendants (2:16).

Heroism at the cost of blood is a theme well known in Jewish history. Rabbi Mordechai of Lachovitch said, "A Jew with no willingness to sacrifice himself is no Jew." But the Hebrew expression for self-sacrifice, *mesirut nefesh*, is most commonly used to designate living self-sacrificially, and likely is what Rabbi Mordechai had in mind.

Those who saw the powerful film *Schindler's List* will recall the tribute paid to Oskar Schindler. He saved hundreds of Jews from the Nazi death camps. Raoul Wallenberg, another such hero of that period, was considered by world Jewry as *khasidey umot ha-olam* (the pious of the world).

The sacrifice of one's life contributes to *kiddush ha-Shem* (sanctification of the Name of God) and has often involved enduring the pangs of death for the honor of God. Jews in the first century would have heard much about such men as Mattathias and his son *Yehudah ha-Maccabee* (Judah the Hammer). Their heroic stand for the honor of "the Name" routed the pagan Syrians from Judea more than a century and a half earlier. That part of history is joyfully brought to mind at the annual festival of *Hanukkah*.

But the memory of Maccabean triumphs over paganism would have also prompted many to ask, "Will the Messiah not lead us to even greater victories against the heathen empire of Rome?"

Hebrews presents an entirely different kind of hero and liberator. His combat is leveled against the unseen powers that debilitate and destroy human life eternally. He has endured the pangs of death that he

24

might fully save us from all the penalty our sins deserve, but not at the expense of compromising the honor of God.

His death satisfied all the Law's righteous demands. His single act of total self-sacrifice forever nullified the power of sin and death. It's no surprise, then, that the writer urged his readers to "consider him" (3:1), that is, deeply concentrate on him, with a view to discern who Yeshua truly was and what he had actually done.

The fullness of his work comes not only as a result of grace, but also as a result of fixing our thoughts upon him. In our fast-paced world, it's not easy to find time for quiet meditation, yet its value is immeasurable when our focus is on "the apostle and High Priest of our confession" (3:1).

CHAPTER FOUR

THE PROMISE OF ENTERING
HIS REST REMAINS
HEBREWS 4:1

HEBREWS 3:1–4:16

In the 1970's, when efforts were being made to reach the Jewish people of New York with Messiah's message, bumper stickers appeared which simply read, "Jews for Moses." The signs were intended to counter the Jews for Jesus organization which was evangelizing on the streets of New York.

This situation was ironic. Moses spoke most definitely about the eventual advent of a greater prophet to whom Israel should carefully listen (Deuteronomy 18:15, 18–19). Yeshua drew his critics' attention to that fact, saying, "If you believed Moses, you would believe me, for he wrote about me" (John 5:46).

Many Jews respectfully refer to the Law bringer as *Moshe rabbenu*, "Moses our teacher." In Maimonides' *Principles of Faith*, Moses is said to have been the greatest of all the prophets, the one who received the Law for Israel and then tirelessly conveyed its contents to the nation through forty years of wandering in the desert. All his words are considered to be absolutely true. Yet the people he led across barren wastelands were called rebellious and stiff-necked, both by the Lord and by the man chosen to lead them (Deuteronomy 9:7–13).

In the final analysis, the greatest of prophets could not effect a change in the hearts of his people. Moses could lead Israel out of Egypt; he could not accomplish a change in their basic tendency to spurn the Law of God. Someone infinitely greater than Moses would be given that task, someone eminently qualified to fulfill God's promise to circumcise the stubborn heart of his people and all mankind (Deuteronomy 30:6).

Nothing is deemed more important than Moses' God-directed teaching regarding *Shabbat*, the Sabbath. In all of Israel's history, nothing has been avoided more than *khilul Shabbat*, desecrating the Sabbath. The Sabbath is referred to affectionately as a "queen." Regulations have been established for properly submitting to her requirements. The mass of laws among the Orthodox is staggering. As one rabbi said, "The rules about the Sabbath...are as mountains hanging by a hair; for Scripture is scanty and the rules many."

There are thirty-nine major types of activities which must be meticulously avoided on *Shabbat*, along with a host of subtypes springing from the larger categories.

It's not just physical work that is shunned, but any activity by which a human influences the environment. This is considered *melakhah*, labor forbidden on the Sabbath. If one is to be *yotse* (meeting the religious requirements), such commonplace actions as turning on a light switch or lighting a match must be avoided.

In Yeshua's day the hundreds of prohibitions often amounted to hair-splitting silliness. For example, one could not "draw a boil" on the Sabbath or carry anything weighing more than two dried figs. Drawing a stick across the ground was considered plowing and was forbidden. A woman was forbidden to pluck a gray hair (better to avoid all mirrors, lest temptation follow the sighting of one). If one arrived at home as the Sabbath commenced, was it permissible to unload his donkey? Could an egg be eaten if it was laid on the Sabbath day, since it was the product of a hen's work? Debates abounded on what was permissible.

Despite the restrictions, the extended day, observed over twenty-five hours, was to be used for all that is spiritually enriching and all that brings rest. It is a time, according to one rabbi, "to praise God and enjoy the best food and drink in the home." On this holy day, Jews greet one another with the words, *Shabbat Shalom*, an expression combining the idea of rest with that of peace, or wholeness.

The Sabbath was intended to be a "delight" and a way to find "joy in the Lord" (Isaiah 58: 13–14). It is a chance to contemplate the great things that God has done, as expressed in this song for the Sabbath:

> *For you make me glad by your deeds, O Lord;*
> *I sing for joy at the works of your hands* (Psalm 92:4).

Israel considered the Sabbath both a mark that distinguished her from other nations and a foretaste of the future days of the Messiah, a time of peace for a troubled world. It is no surprise, therefore, that the prayer known as *havdalah* (separation) closes each Sabbath-day's worship:

> *Praise be to you, O Lord our God, King of the World, who does distinguish the sacred from the profane, the light from the darkness, Israel from all other nations and the seventh day from the days of work.*

Although the prayer celebrated God's creation of the blessed day, *Talmudic* scholars taught that if all the people kept the Sabbath rigorously, God's messianic redemption would quickly follow. Thus the people's works, rather than God's works, soon occupied center stage.

Nothing made the Pharisees angrier with Yeshua than what they considered to be his gross disregard for laws governing the Sabbath. Although he could regularly be found in the synagogue where he read and taught Scripture on *Shabbat*, his detractors believed he was continually flouting the laws concerning this sacred day.

In point of fact, the institution of the Sabbath had come to be unduly exalted, even against a rabbinical warning, "The Sabbath is given over to you, but you are not given over to the Sabbath. Yeshua stated the same truth more concisely: "The Sabbath was made for man, not man for the Sabbath" (Mark 2:27).

The Hebrew believers recalled that the Pharisees' chief criticism about Yeshua's Sabbath "violations" pertained to his healing the sick. Although the *Tenakh* did not forbid healing on the Sabbath, the rabbis considered healing to be work and therefore permissible only if an individual's life were at stake.

Yeshua could often be observed healing the chronically afflicted and handicapped on the Sabbath. On one occasion the eyewitness to the healing of a man with a shriveled hand reported that Yeshua was "deeply distressed at the stubborn hearts" of those present who would not speak supportively of his compassionate miracle (Mark 3:4–5).

But if human compassion would not support Yeshua's acts of kindness, a higher authority would. The master taught that all of his acts were, in truth, a direct expression of the Father's love for his people. Yeshua only did what he saw his father doing (John 5:19).

Yeshua stressed how appropriate the act of healing was on the Sabbath, pointing to the redemptive significance of that day. Had not the Law commanded Israel to keep the Sabbath in remembrance of the fact that God had broken their cruel chains?

> *Remember that you were slaves in Egypt and that the Lord brought you out of there with a strong hand and an outstretched arm. Therefore the Lord your God has commanded you to observe the Sabbath day* (Deuteronomy 5:15) .

The same mighty Lord who had freed the captives was doing it once more, now breaking Satan's spiritual hold on souls and delivering the physically handicapped and diseased.

How appropriate for the sick to be healed on the Sabbath, as Yeshua's deeds and declaration revealed: "Should not this woman, a daughter of Abraham, whom Satan has kept bound for eighteen long years, be set free on the Sabbath day from what bound her?" (Luke 13:10–16).

Yeshua further affirmed his right to release the oppressed by virtue of the fact that he was "Lord of the Sabbath," leaving no doubt about the divinity of him through whom all things were made (Matthew 12:1–8, see John 1:3, Hebrews 1:2).

Hebrews reminds us that there is more than one dimension to our Sabbath rest, since neither Moses nor his successor, Joshua, could provide God's full measure of rest for Israel. "There remains, then, a Sabbath rest for the people of God" (4:9).

The Jewish writer to the Hebrew believers brought two themes together in order to make exceptionally clear what the Messiah had accomplished. The first of these themes involved creation.

God ceased from his work and gave the seventh day as an eternal marker showing that not by works, but by faith, could one enter into his completed work. "We who have believed enter that rest..." (4:3). Moses, in his Genesis narrative, recorded no evening for the seventh day of creation, revealing that it is finished, yet open, an unending blessedness for all who would trustingly receive God's invitation. In a somewhat startling statement, the Father speaks of his own "refreshment" on the seventh day (Exodus 31:17) and invites his people to be refreshed as well.

The second theme deals with redemption. God enabled his dearly beloved to "rest" in Canaan, the result of a redemptive miracle. Now God's great redemptive sign-post, the Lord Yeshua the Messiah, gives an invitation to a heavenly gathering where one may fully sing "the song of Moses the servant of God and the song of the Lamb" (Revelation 15:3).

Yeshua is God's Sabbath rest for all who will trust in his finished work. He becomes the focal point of rest by virtue of his having been "sacrificed once to take away the sins of many people" (9:28).

As early as the first century, the friendly greeting *"shalom alechem"* ("peace upon you") would bring the response *"alechem shalom"* ("upon you peace"). The word *shalom* also referred to a finished product; in fact, when the last stone of Solomon's Temple was in place, many Jews spoke of the building as *shalom*, complete.

31

No greater theme was ever expressed to the people of God than that which proclaimed their wholeness, their true *shalom*, in the Messiah. The rabbis correctly believed that *Shalom* was one of God's names, for Isaiah's prophecy called him *Sar Shalom*, Prince of Peace (Isaiah 9:6). Now the wholeness of God became available, "For he is our peace" (Ephesians 2:14). Those who trust him have become a completed building, a holy temple in which his spirit dwells (Ephesians 2:22).

This clear word of peace, of comfort, is counterbalanced by a compelling challenge: "Let us, therefore, make every effort to enter that rest..." (4:11). The readers of this epistle realized that God's rest contained both present and future blessings.

"Now," they are being told, "you may enter into God's rest by trusting in the Messiah's finished work on your behalf." Yet it doesn't end there. We also need to consider our prospects: the Messiah has gone into heaven itself (9:11) where the fulfillment of rest awaits us. Think about it. That rest which he has already prepared should encourage each one to stand fast in their commitment to Yeshua.

The writer of Hebrews pointed out that unbelief always separated man from God's rest. The generation traversing the wilderness drew God's displeasure," ...they would never enter his rest" (3:18–19). But it is no encouragement to hear such words if they don't drive us to perseverance.

In Israel the Orthodox have always loved the expression, *be-ezrat ha-Shem* ("With the help of the Name [of God]"). The readers of this epistle were reminded that God knew all about their obstacles, how difficult their life was, and that he viewed their situation with the utmost sympathy (4:15). What the Jewish believer cannot do himself (cleave to God's promises at all times), he can trust God to enable him to do: *be-ezrat ha-Shem*. He wrote that "we may receive mercy and find grace to help us in our time of need" (4:16).

Moreover, God had given his people the potential for a vibrant fellowship. Together, they could encourage one another with their redeemer's promises, "day by day" (3:13).

God did not want his people to live on tenterhooks, wondering if the next personal crisis would sever their relationship with him. Mes-

siah, who takes the initiative by inviting sinners to come to him for
support, "always lives to intercede for them" (7:25).

In calling Yeshua an "apostle" (3:1) the writer will have been aware
of the word's Hebrew counterpart, *sheliakh*. The rabbis taught that "the
one who is sent" (*sheliakh*) is the same as the one who sends. Although
it originated in the area of legal representation, it accurately identified him who is God's "exact representation" (1:3). This should mo-
tivate us further to fix our thoughts on Yeshua, who is worthy of the
greatest honor.

CHAPTER FIVE

LET US THEN APPROACH THE THRONE OF GRACE WITH CONFIDENCE
HEBREWS 4:16

HEBREWS 4:1–16

There are many types of prayer in Jewish religious life. The silent prayer, called *Amidah*, is recited while standing. Though uttered under one's breath, it is still an intense plea for help, for blessing, for peace, for direction.

There is a prayer which seeks the alleviation of suffering. It is prayed from a sitting position, perhaps with the head drooping down or the body bent over.

During the High Holy Days, *Rosh HaShanah* (the Feast of Trumpets and Jewish New Year) and *Yom Kippur* (the Day of Atonement), the *Avinu Malkenu* (Our Father, our King) beseeches God's support and asks him to avenge those who have been wronged: "...act on behalf of those who have gone through fire and water to sanctify your name...avenge the spilt blood..."

There are special prayers during the feast of *Sukkot* when the wilderness wanderings are commemorated. Each day worshippers begin their supplication with the word *Hoshanah*, "Save, we plead."

There are regularly scheduled times when Jews band together to pray—morning, afternoon, and evening. The shortest of these (requiring only a few minutes) comes mid-day and is called *Minkhah* (gift), and may help direct a busy Jew's thoughts to the source of his livelihood. The evening prayers are usually said at dusk in the synagogue.

The religious Jew begins each day with the words *modeh ani*, the prayer meaning "I thank you, living eternal King; for in mercy you have restored my soul to me. Great is your trustworthiness."

Like so many other prayers, those offered on fast days ask God not to focus on our wickedness but, rather, on his mercy. Often the prayers are accompanied by symbolic acts.

Each new year begins by Jews gathering by a river, stream, or shore to symbolically cast their sins into the water. The promise of the prophet Micah is remembered: "You will again have compassion on us; you will tread our sins underfoot and hurl all our iniquities into the depths of the sea" (Micah 7:19). The cleansing ceremony is known as *tashlikh*, Hebrew for "hurl."

Several days later, on *Yom Kippur*, the prayer known as *Kol Nidrey* (All Vows) offers these words to God: "All vows, oaths, and resolutions of any kind [between us and God]...we hereby renounce and declare null and void: our vows shall be nonvows, our oaths nonoaths, and our resolutions nonresolutions." This ancient prayer—still said in the original Aramaic language—dates from a time when Jews, in order to avoid torture and death, were compelled to accept other faiths. Yet beyond the release of this kind of vow, there exists a deeper desire—to be released from those commandments which reveal our faithlessness before the God whose awesome holiness terrifies us in our ungodliness.

In the Gospel of Luke, Yeshua compares two contrasting acts of prayer. In order to fully understand the meaning of the story, we need to consider the context of Israel's worship. "Two men went up into the Temple to pray." Luke 18:10 is speaking about two individuals who go to engage in corporate worship. They went to a place designated for that purpose, the Temple. They went up at the same time; and they will leave at the same time, at the service's conclusion.

Historically, for the Jewish community, collective worship is every bit as important as anything one does privately. In Yeshua's day Temple rituals involved a morning and evening sacrifice at which many would gather to worship.

Although each prays privately, they are part of a larger company who have gone to the Temple to worship, to pray (perhaps most intensely during the burning of incense), and to receive the Aaronic benediction from Israel's appointed priest.

Apart from the elaborate rituals connected with the services, the most significant element in both the early morning and mid-afternoon worship was the sacrifice of a lamb for the people's sins. At dawn, the smoke from the sacrifice rose above the altar and Temple area. Everyone who came to worship would be conscious of the burning, the smoke, the fragrance the atonement which made it possible for him, a sinner, to address a holy God.

At three in the afternoon, the offering was replenished and burnt. The altar reminded the worshipper of the centrality of sacrifice and the provision for access to God.

We know much about Pharisees and tax-collectors, including their mutual disdain toward each other. The Pharisees' attention to the details of the Law as well as their attitude towards tax collectors, including the *am ha-aretz*, the "people of the land," is well documented.

Of course anyone could legitimately find fault with the tax collector. Linking him with robbers and evil-doers (perhaps even the "extortionists" and the "unjust") was no exaggeration (Luke 18:11).

The Pharisee utters the word, "adulterers," too. This is not necessarily leveled at the tax-collector, but in this way the Pharisee elevates himself still further above the corrupt humanity around him.

Yeshua tells us that both men are standing; each of them occupies a place remote from others, but for vastly different reasons.

For the Pharisee to come into contact with the *am ha-aretz* would bring *midras* (uncleanness). The rulings of the *Mishnah* (the first part of the *Talmud*) declared that the Pharisee would become unclean even if he brushed against the clothes of someone like a tax-collector. And lest someone else in the company of worshippers be of ill-repute, aloofness safeguarded against the sin of becoming ceremonially tainted.

In *Mere Christianity*, C.S. Lewis makes the point that, although sins of the flesh are bad, all the worst sins are purely spiritual: the pleasure of controlling others, pleasures of power, of hatred, of putting others down. These beneath-the-surface sins are, regrettably, ingrained in each of us.

Jewish practice was to pray aloud. Probably the Pharisee's "prayer" was audible and, in some sense, his words were intended to instruct the "less righteous" in his vicinity. *Talmudic* scholars spoke critically of the "shoulder" Pharisee, who took pains to make everyone aware of his piety, wearing, as it were, his piety on his shoulders.

A gong would sound at the time of the offering of incense in the Holy Place. It was then customary for those considered unclean to stand and, if necessary, be ushered to the Temple's eastern gate. The tax-collector needed no "escort" to a more remote place. He stood afar off from the very beginning of this time of prayer (Luke 18:13).

The Pharisee boasts that he is not only superior to others but has actually exceeded the demands of the Law. Although in citing his accomplishments he doesn't compare himself to figures like Abraham or Samuel (we're usually quite careful in selecting those with whom we'll compare ourselves) he must think that he measures up fairly well against Israel's spiritual giants.

He goes beyond the annual fast on *Yom Kippur* that all Jews are required to keep and is part of a select company. He would have referred to them as *khaverim* (associates). They abstain from food twice weekly. Tradition said that Moses ascended Sinai on a Monday and descended on a Thursday. These were probably the fast days chosen by the Pharisees.

In addition, he focused carefully on the *ma'aser* (tithe). Rabbi Gamaliel, the apostle Paul's teacher, said, "Do not often tithe by conjecture." That is, don't make it a matter of guesswork. Religious Jews took the instruction quite seriously.

Still today it is the practice of the Orthodox Jews to reserve a tithe from Israel's produce. In Yeshua's day, the idea of tithing nonagricultural items was just beginning to emerge. This Pharisee had already established a plan for dealing with such products.

Here, then, is a Pharisee (there were more righteous Pharisees, too, such as Nicodemus and Paul) who fit well into a group who were "confident of their own righteousness and looked down on everybody else" (Luke 18:9), a person who might assume he was always welcome in God's presence.

More than seven centuries earlier, Isaiah considered the kinds of people who engaged in what he called *mitzvot anashim melumadah* (rules made up and taught by men), rote and meaningless religiosity. They appeared to draw near to God with the words of their mouth, but their hearts remained at a distance (Isaiah 29:13).

Yeshua said that Isaiah was accurately prophesying of the Pharisees, who were so indifferent to the claims of genuine religion. They were the "blind guides" so resistant to his teachings (Matthew 15:7–9, 14).

Our attention is then drawn to a man full of self-loathing. His self-deprecation is not without reason. He has been a traitor to his people, a Jew who sold out to Rome, a crook by any standard. He has no confidence before God. His eyes are turned downward and, in the traditional Jewish attitude of repentance, he beats his chest.

A weakness of conventional Judaism has been its attention to sins rather than to man's fallenness. Because the heart is hopelessly diseased, a radical cure must be found if man's relationship with God is to be healed, if man is to approach God with confidence.

The publican can only cry out, "God, be merciful to me, the sinner" (Luke 18:13). The verb "be merciful" means "be propitiated." Let your wrath be removed from me.

Hebrews 2:17 states that Yeshua is a merciful and faithful High Priest in service to God and that he made atonement an act of propitiation for the sins of the people. "Let that atonement count for me," the tax collector pleads. "Let what is done there upon the altar pronounce me clean in your sight."

Like the Pharisee, he has placed himself within a class of people. But he numbers himself with those who are needy and see themselves under condemnation in the light of God's holiness. They deserve nothing but God's wrath.

The Pharisee senses no need for mercy. He leaves the Temple's precincts under the delusion—fed by legalism—that all is well between him and God. He has asked for nothing; he received what he asked for.

The tax collector has asked for mercy, the only thing he dared ask for; and he has received the benefits from the altar. He returns home "justified," "righteous," "acquitted of his sins." By grace he has been "exalted."

It is God's unique prerogative to elevate a person; Yeshua's authoritative teaching on the subject is the same as the prophet Ezekiel's: "The lowly will be exalted and the exalted will be brought low" (Ezekiel 21:26). To be exalted is to be lifted up in relation to God. The Messianic believers had access to God for they were brought near his throne through the blood of the Messiah.

Augustine taught that God only gives where he finds empty hands. A person with their hands full of parcels can't receive a gift. Righteousness, the key that opens the door to fellowship with God, cannot be received just by rigorous attention to keeping the Law.

We must come with remorse, humbly confessing our sin and fix our hope on the altar of sacrifice where full atonement has been made. There, and there alone, will our great High Priest welcome us.

Could my zeal no respite know,
Could my tears forever flow,
All for sin could not atone;
Thou must save, and Thou alone.
                                    A.M.Toplady

CHAPTER SIX

HE LEARNED OBEDIENCE
FROM WHAT HE SUFFERED
HEBREWS 5:8

HEBREWS 5:1–14

Perhaps the most important aspect of sonship in Jewish tradition comes to a boy when he turns thirteen. At that time, following personal study under his rabbi's direction, he is declared to be a *bar mitzvah*, a son of the commandment.

Much rejoicing occurs, especially for the boy's parents whose son has now become a man in the eyes of the synagogue. In Orthodoxy, it is a time for the father to relinquish control, to commend his son more fully to the direct oversight of God Almighty. From the young man's standpoint, he now considers himself responsible to keep the full requirements of the Law. In modern times there is a similar celebration for girls at twelve. But *bat mitzvah* is not practiced by the very Orthodox.

When I "became a man" in the eyes of my elders, I received a certificate from the synagogue on which was printed, "We will hearken and we will do!" Based on the response of the Israelites to Moses' proclamation of the will of the LORD (Exodus 19:8), it was a verse chosen for me, but one I failed to take seriously due to its extensive demands. Judging from my people's history, their words far exceeded their deeds.

My teenage years were characterized by a lack of concern for the *mitzvot*. As far as the demands of *Torah* were concerned, I was an abject failure.

As I passed into my twenties, my times of religious reflection were generally periods of discouragement, for while my peers considered me to be one of the *b'nai b'rit* (sons of the covenant), my heart made me aware that I was nothing more than a covenant breaker. And with each passing year, my relationship with God seemed to lessen.

Our ancient tradition tells of a *melitz yosher*, a pleader of righteousness, who speaks before heaven's tribunal in defense of those in the world. Tombs of the deceased who were considered to have been godly are frequented by worshippers asking God to accept their intercessory petitions.

The Hebrew believers were comforted that they had one "appointed to represent them in matters related to God" (5:1). They had no need to worry about the effectiveness of his advocacy, for God had chosen him to serve as eternal High Priest (5:4–6). Two Psalms are quoted to reassure them: Psalm 2, in which the close relationship between the Father and the Son is established ("You are my Son..."), and Psalm 110, where a divine oath confirms the Messiah as a priest eternally enthroned.

There is a special quality to Messiah's intercession by virtue of what the Hebrews called his *rakhmanut* (compassion). The depth of his care for us is revealed by the word's root, *rekhem*, which refers to a mother's womb. His compassion runs deep because of the suffering he has endured; he has personally experienced grief in its most violent forms.

When the writer tells his people that their pioneer was made perfect through suffering (2:10), he is in no sense suggesting that there was any moral imperfection in God's Anointed. Rather he is showing that Yeshua had become perfectly suited to the demanding work of his priestly office. His suitability is linked to his ability to empathize fully with those who suffer.

Another element in the Messiah's "progression" to the point of priestly perfection involves his obedience. Although the Messiah entered this world without the taint of sin, it remained for his innocence to be tested thoroughly. If the savior of men was to stand in their place as a righteous offering he would first have to show that he totally embraced the commands of the *Torah*. Only his total obedience would qualify him to offer himself up on our behalf; only then could one man's obedience declare many righteous (Romans 5:19).

His total submission to the Law's demands would bring intense sorrow as he acquired, by experience, the knowledge of obedience. The Gospels record Yeshua's severe testing in the wilderness when he is goaded to use his Messianic powers in a self-serving manner. Only Mark gives no account of that intense confrontation between the Messiah and the devil. Perhaps Mark knew that Yeshua's entire life was characterized by testing, not only by Satan, but also by people and events facing him every day.

The determination to retain his integrity is never more apparent than during the night in the garden of Gethsemane. Yeshua "offered up prayers and petitions with loud cries and tears to the One who could save him from death..."(5:7). The rabbis spoke of three types of praying: silently communing with God, crying out to God, and weeping before him. The last of these types was deemed most precious in the Almighty's sight. All of these Yeshua knew in the lonely darkness when "his sweat was as drops of blood falling to the ground" (Luke 22:44).

Yeshua was heard by his father (5:7). The Messiah's godly reverence brought forth an answer: "An angel from heaven appeared to him and strengthened him" (Luke 22:43) that he might endure the otherwise unendurable. As the Master recoiled from the horror of becoming a sin offering and enduring the pollution of his people's transgressions, he nonetheless refused to shrink back from drinking that bitter cup to its dregs.

Centuries before, prophet after prophet had spoken of God's "cup of wrath" that all the ungodly would be compelled to drink (Jeremiah 25, Habakkuk 2:16, Ezekiel 23, Isaiah 51). To drink that terrible cup was the result of divine judgment, a judgment whose sweeping devastation would consume all the godless, even those whose history had yet to be written (Revelation 14:9–11). Those forced to consume the wine of God's fury would be destroyed by it: they would "fall and rise no more" (Jeremiah 25:27). It was that awful, incalculably severe wrath, the contemplation of which caused Yeshua to cry out, "Father, if you are willing, take this cup from me..." (Luke 22:42).

Jerusalem, the holy city, headed the list of those who would drink from the LORD's dreadful cup (Jeremiah 25:18). Writing in the *midrash*, Rabbi Yochanan said, "Jerusalem will one day be the capital of the world." But the city of David, though her name contains the word *shalom*, cannot hope to know true peace without her righteous king.

Here is a prayer of unknown origin that used to appear in versions of the *Makhzor*, the Jewish prayer book used during the High Holy Days (*Rosh HaShanah* and *Yom Kippur*). It suggests that some of our people knew the truth about Messiah:

> [The] *righteous Messiah has departed from us;*
> *We are horror-stricken and there is none to justify us;*
> *Our iniquities and the yoke of our transgression*
> *He carries and is wounded for our transgressions.*
> *He bears on His shoulders our sins to find pardon*
> *For our iniquities*
> *May we be healed by His stripes.*

There are many *selikhot* (prayers for forgiveness) in the Jewish tradition, but believers in God's Messiah have learned that the cost of that forgiveness is higher than anyone had previously imagined: the obedient suffering and death of God's only son.

Yeshua, the Messiah, has become "the source of eternal salvation for all who obey him" (5:9). His salvation is not, therefore, a slap-dash whitewashing of the sins of every living soul. His sacrifice requires a personal response, even the obedience of faith through which "we who believe enter that rest" (4:3). We cannot know his love unless our souls cleave to him.

The Jewish believers were not only being reminded of the depths of their savior's love; they were also being instructed about their own spiritual development. By grace, through faith, they had become members of the Messiah's household, his *mishpakhah*. He is delighted to call them "family" (2:11).

His life serves both to save us from the consequences of our sins and to show us the meaning of true obedience. Qualities such as humility, patience, submissiveness, and endurance under extreme pressure are no more popular today than they were in the first century when those who trusted in the Messiah were called upon to follow his example.

To whom much is given, much is also expected. "If any man would come after me let him deny himself and take up his cross and follow me" (Matthew 16:24). In the struggle to follow Messiah, God will strengthen his child, even as he supported his very own son during that exceedingly dark night of his soul.

There was no easy path ahead for those believers; and our path may prove to be equally severe. But God has promised, "Never will I leave you; never will I forsake you" (13:5).

The words of C.S. Lewis offer us this true solace: "If and when a horror turns up you will then be given grace to help you." One is not usually given this grace in advance. "Give us our daily bread" (not an annuity for life) applies to spiritual gifts too. That daily support sustains us for our daily trials.

Life has to be taken day by day and hour by hour. "So we say with confidence, 'The Lord is my helper; I will not be afraid. What can man do to me?'"(13:6). After all, "God is faithful; he will not let you be tempted beyond what you can bear. But when you are tempted [tested], he will also provide a way out so that you can stand up under it" (1 Corinthians 10:13).

CHAPTER SEVEN

WE HAVE THIS HOPE AS AN
ANCHOR FOR THE SOUL
HEBREWS 6:19

HEBREWS 6:1–20

I stopped making promises to God many years ago. As a troubled (and sometimes troublesome) teenager I recall meeting with my rabbi and pledging my obedience to God in order that I might never again be an embarrassment to my family or the God of my fathers. Up to that point, I had been rebelliously insensitive to them both.

My university professor suggested I attend to what was colloquially referred to as *Perek, The Ethics of the Fathers*. But, in truth, I desired no wise sayings, no voice from the past with good advice.

A prudent instructor challenges his student to be honest about that which he does not understand, to say, "I do not understand." To all who would listen, I was saying just that: "I do not understand." Can I personally know the God of Abraham, Isaac, and Jacob or must my knowledge of him be confined to the Law he has commanded me to obey? If obedience to the Law was going to determine my future, then I was indeed without hope. Maxims and the sayings of sages could not salvage a vessel fast taking on water and about to capsize.

A son of Korah knew God to be his refuge and strength, an ever-present help, so he could say, "...we will not fear though the earth give way and the mountains fall into the heart of the sea..." (Psalm 46:1–2). But where could refuge for my soul be found? I was adrift in a sea of inner turmoil with no stabilizing ballast. Grace, that most wonderful truth, would finally bring stability to my life.

An anchor is a symbol of hope. Hope, like an anchor, keeps a person from drifting; it steadies him in the midst of the currents of life. "Pay more careful attention," the Hebrews are told, "so that we do not drift away" (2:1).

For this son of Israel, the time had finally come to dedicate myself to the study of the Scriptures. Whereas my previous efforts were half-hearted, I was now engaged in a desperate search for spiritual reality, a quest for *khizuk* (encouragement). It was grace that compelled me to read; and as I read I prayed, "O God of Abraham, Isaac, and Jacob, please reveal yourself to me." He answered my plea and graciously helped me to know him by trusting in his many reliable promises.

Encouragement for the Hebrews came through remembering how God dealt with Abraham. His spiritual beginning was bound up with promises made to him by God in Genesis: "I will make you into a great nation...I will make your name great...and all peoples on earth will be blessed through you" (Genesis 12:2–3). The promise was enlarged upon in Genesis 17 when God, identifying himself as *El Shaddai* (God Almighty), promised to establish his covenant with Abraham and his descendants for all generations to come.

I could not help but notice the miracle attached to the promise of a "vast progeny," for Abraham was an old man and laughingly called attention to that fact: "Will a son be born to a man a hundred years old?" (Genesis 17:17). When Abraham considered that his wife's age was ninety, it only further discouraged him about the fulfillment of the promise.

As I read those words I understood that I, like multitudes who have read that text, would have to deal with the question which faced the patriarch as well: "Is God capable of doing the thing he has committed himself to do?"

Since the earliest of times, my people have confessed that *YHVH*, the LORD, is *Adon Olam, Ribono shel Olam* (Lord of the Universe, Master of the Universe), yet in practice we rely too much on our own wits to alter and improve our circumstances. Even Abraham succumbed to that natural tendency more than once (Genesis 12:10–13; 16:1–2).

Abraham had already expressed his faith in God's promised *b'rakhot* (blessings) when he left Ur of the Chaldees, where he undoubtedly owned considerable property. Soon afterwards, he took hold of God's promise to give him, an aging patriarch, a son from his very own loins. "Abraham believed the LORD, and [the LORD] credited it to him as righteousness" (Genesis 15:6).

We are never given the details of Abraham's conversion, but his reliance on the LORD, especially in times of crisis, was of critical importance. The Hebrew believers were enduring great hardship and needed "to show this same diligence to the very end..." (6:11). They needed "faith and patience" to "inherit what was promised" (6:12). Again and again the Genesis narrative spoke of God's weighty promises to Abraham until, after Abraham willingly offered up Isaac, God added a new element—his personal oath:

> *The angel of the Lord called to Abraham...and said, 'I swear by myself, declares the Lord, that because you have...not withheld your son, your only begotten son, I will surely bless you...* (Genesis 22:15–16).

There are two unchangeable truths—God's promise and his oath—on which the Hebrews continually rested (6:18). When Abraham "believed" God's word, he leaned upon it as his foundation (Genesis 15:6).

The word translated faith, *emunah*, not only defines Abraham's trust but is the root word for the well-known derivative, *amen*. It was this fundamental word, denoting reliance upon God, which Maimonides, in his *Principles of Faith*, taught all Jews to say, "I believe with perfect faith in the coming of the Messiah, and though he delay yet shall I wait for him."

The solemnity of this statement, uttered by Jews even as they went to death in the Nazi gas chambers, has an oath like quality. It resounds in hope that God will fulfill his promise to send *Mashiakh*. The Hebrew believers had spoken their "Amen!" to the witness of that fulfillment in Yeshua. Now they needed to trust solely in the faithfulness of his person and word.

When we read that God made a covenant we are really reading the Hebrew idiom, *karat b'rit*, that he "cut a covenant." God's covenants were literally "cut." Blood was shed as an essential part of all such agreements.

The sacrifices spoke both to the gravity of sin and to God's covenanted measures to counteract sin's consequences. Because of the sinfulness of humanity, the pledge to obey, however well meant, must be made being cognizant of God's provision for forgiveness; so the altar is sprinkled, along with the people, with the blood of the covenant.

When the LORD entered into a covenant relationship with Abraham, "a terror and a great darkness" overshadowed the solemn event (Genesis 15:12). God, represented as a blazing furnace, passed between slain animals. By so doing, the LORD was ratifying his covenant for Abraham's sake, respecting the Near Eastern traditions of that day. This profound symbolic action said, in effect, "May the curse befalling these victims come upon me if I am at all unfaithful to my promises."

Abraham was a passive recipient of the covenanted blessings as God passed between the dismembered animals. The patriarch was not asked to repeat the solemn ritual which, if he were ever unfaithful, could forever seal his doom. This covenant was made unilaterally.

A disconcerting prophecy also accompanied the divinely-made covenant: "Your descendants will be strangers in a country not their own and they will be enslaved and mistreated four hundred years" (Genesis 15:13). It happened as God said; but the people were not forgotten, "For he remembered his holy promise given to his servant Abraham.

He brought his people out with rejoicing, his chosen ones with shouts of joy" (Psalm 105:42–43). God's delays do not signify denials; we and the Hebrews are linked to one who is "faithful and true" (Revelation 19:11).

After their liberation from Egypt the Israelites were dramatically reminded of the basis for their salvation. We read of Moses building an altar:

> *Then...they offered burnt offerings and fellowship offerings to the LORD. Moses took half of the blood and put it in bowls, and the other half he sprinkled on the altar...Moses then took the blood, sprinkled it on the people and said, "This is the blood of the covenant that the LORD has made with you...."* (Exodus 24: 5–8).

In between these acts the people heard the words of God and responded, "We will do everything the LORD has said; we will obey" (Genesis 24:7). No matter how sincere the pledge, the sinfulness of the nation required that the promise also be ratified with God's provision for forgiveness. For this reason, the altar is sprinkled along with the people with the blood of the covenant.

The passage of time never altered this essential foundation for God's dealings with fallen man: sin required the forfeiture of life. As I began to read the Scriptures one fixed principle remained evident. Ultimately, the Spirit pointed me to him whose precious blood has the power to "sprinkle many nations" (Isaiah 52:15).

Synagogues are constructed to remind the Jew of the ancient Temple, a more ornate version of the tabernacle in the wilderness. There is a *parokhet* (curtain) drawn across the place where the sacred *Torah* scrolls are kept. It is a reminder of the veil which separated the people from the Holy of Holies. Much ritual accompanies the opening of this veil and the reading of the Scriptures. How unlike its ancient counterpart, where, behind the *parokhet* resided not only the *aron kodesh* (holy ark), but also the *sh'khinah*, the manifest presence of God.

The hope of which Hebrews speaks is a vital hope because it allows the believer to enter the inner sanctuary where God dwells. The vast body of Jewish law, known as *halakhah* (the way), can never usher us into the presence of God; only he who is the Way makes such communion possible. To all who have ever known the frustrating burden of attempting to enter by any other route, the words of Hebrews are a comfort: "We have this hope as a sure and safe anchor for ourselves, a hope that goes right on through to what is inside the *parokhet*" (6:19).

CHAPTER EIGHT

SUCH A HIGH PRIEST MEETS OUR NEEDS
HEBREWS 7:26

HEBREWS 7

Throughout the letter to the Jewish believers, no point receives as much attention as the Messiah's priesthood. Hebrews is the only New Testament document which actually calls him our great High Priest. More than forty percent of the epistle deals with some aspect of his intercessory ministry.

In this context one figure from Israel's past captured the attention of the writer—Melchizedek, "king of Salem and a priest of God most high" (7:1). The name *Malkhi-tzedek* combines *melekh* (king) and *tzedek* (righteousness). The brief appearance of this person on the stage of patriarchal history (Genesis 14:18–20) would seem too insignificant to deserve the kind of extended attention found here. Yet Melchizedek's name and function provide rich, supportive insights for the believer.

One of Israel's most lamentable moments occurred when Uzziah, Judah's otherwise capable and gifted monarch, tried to usurp the position of priest. Presumptuously, he entered the Temple to offer incense on the altar. His pride led to God's swift judgment. He was immediately stricken with leprosy and lived in isolation until the day he died (2 Chronicles 26:16–21).

No individual since the time of Melchizedek received God's sanction to occupy both distinctly separate offices of king and priest. There was, however, David's prophetic text which anticipated a messianic Priest-King: Psalm 110. From earliest times, Jewish people have believed that David wrote this psalm in honor of the Messiah. The first century Pharisees, not to mention the society at Qumran, were among those who championed this interpretation. It is for good reason the most frequently quoted psalm in the New Testament.

At the very least, David points to a figure of a nature superior to his own. If one takes the clear meaning of the text—what we call the *peshat*—David's words regarding the exaltation of the Messiah would be inappropriate were the reference to a mere mortal:

"The LORD said to Adonai," begins the text (Psalm 110:1). David is saying that God has spoken to David's Lord about a certain matter: "Sit at my right hand until I make your enemies a footstool for your feet." This is an invitation to reign with "God most high" (7:1).

In Hebrew exposition the rabbis speak of the *d'rash*, the applied meaning of a Biblical verse. Here we read of a kingly Messiah whose domain (mighty scepter) cannot be contained within Zion (which like the word Salem is another way of referring to Jerusalem). His rule even encompasses territories where Messiah's adversaries dwell (Psalm 110:2).

In the words of the psalmist, then, an incontestable foundation is laid for the coming of one whose reign has divine dimensions. He is "arrayed in the beauties of holiness" (Psalm 110:3).

My conviction is that when Isaiah saw the vision of his uplifted Lord (Isaiah 6:1), the vision was of Messiah. This explains why John's quote from Isaiah 6 is accompanied by that disciple's bold declaration that Isaiah "saw Yeshua's glory and spoke about him" (John 12:39–41).

The idea of Messiah's priestliness has not been part of Jewish thought. Yochanan ben Zakkai spoke for the majority when he said, "If you should have a sapling in your hand when they tell you that the Messiah has arrived, first plant the sapling and then go to greet the Messiah." In other words, the Messiah has simply come to usher in a kingdom of peace and beauty.

Modern Jewish thought has largely jettisoned the idea of a personal Messiah. The prevailing view of liberal Judaism envisions the world ultimately perfected through the influence of the two Judaic ideals of justice and compassion. Of course, that hope ignores the teaching of Scripture with respect to the plight of fallen man, and substitutes humanistic thinking for heaven's miraculous intervention.

When I first spoke with my rabbi about my faith in Yeshua the Messiah he said, in effect, "If he is the Messiah, how is it that the world is still in such chaos?" He went on to point out that since he was a trained theologian and I was not, it was useless to debate the matter.

He was curious to learn, however, what I had experienced to bring me to this conviction? I was nervous as I stood before him; but I was able to account for what had happened in my life on the basis of what the writer to the Hebrews said of Yeshua:

"A better hope has been introduced by which we may draw near to God....Such a High Priest meets our need...He sacrificed for our sins once and for all when he offered up himself" (7:19, 26–27).

Each man must come to grips with the fact that he is a sinner. For Isaiah, the problem was *nibul peh* (fouling the mouth). His speech made him particularly conscious of sin (Isaiah 6:5). Standing in God's presence, while aware of his foulness, was the height of personal pain for Isaiah. *Nidmeyti!* he cried. "I am destroyed!"

Priestly intervention was the LORD's appointed means to give sinners access to their holy God. For Isaiah, his exalted priest had made provision for the prophet at the altar. No greater words of comfort were ever heard than those which quieted his troubled soul: "See...your guilt is taken away and your sin atoned for" (Isaiah 6:7).

Here was a sinner who, by virtue of the altar's power, could stand in the presence of the Holy One of Israel. Those who know Messiah may hear the same benediction every time they look toward him in need. No one who hopes in God's saving power need ever fear his rejection.

Did the teachers of Israel understand the link between the righteousness of Messiah and his kingdom of peace? The psalmist saw the connection between the two when he said: "righteousness and peace have kissed one another" (Psalm 85:10). A son of Korah observed this harmony as he reflected on the fruits of atonement: "You forgave the iniquity of your people and covered all their sins" (Psalm 85:2).

In Yeshua's day the word *tzedakah* (righteousness) had often received a fairly narrow interpretation at the hands of the Pharisees. From their perspective, the giving of alms, prayer and fasting were the most important aspects of righteousness (note this in Luke 18, especially, in the behavior of the Pharisee at the Temple).

Oddly enough, "almsgiving" had actually become a synonym for *tzedakah*. To think that by giving charity one might become righteous in God's sight—even earning one's salvation—surely gave rise to Yeshua's warning: "Unless your righteousness exceeds that of the Pharisees...you will certainly not enter the kingdom of heaven" (Matthew 5:20). All have minuscule "righteousness" before the judge of heaven.

While the Pharisees knew that "righteousness" could be a synonym for "salvation," they failed to realize that only "the LORD is our righteousness" (Jeremiah 23:6). There is no hope for salvation apart from trusting in the provision of the Messiah, "king of righteousness" (7:2). "To seek first the kingdom of God and his righteousness" (Matthew 6:33) means, above all else, to seek a relationship with him "who is able to save completely those who come to God through him" (7:25).

The *Tenakh*, the Old Testament, had its mediators, but no absolute guarantors of personal salvation. In Messiah, each one may find his soul's "surety" (7:22).

What my synagogue held out to me as an obligation—"we will hearken and obey"— exceeded my ability. Yeshua has fulfilled my obligation perfectly. He is answerable on my behalf for all of the Law's requirements including its dreaded penalty of death (Ezekiel 18:4).

In time, all of us must contend with the pain of separation and loss. We look back and wonder why we did not do better in our relationships, or try harder to follow the principles that we know would make our lives more fulfilling. But no matter how hard we try to follow the Law, it can never perfect us (7:19). Only by personally trusting in our relationship with Messiah are we linked to that unconquerable "better hope...by which we draw near to God" (7:18).

Israel's relation to the Messiah, like the relationship of the moon to the sun, was to reflect his glory. He was not exalted by the Law—Moses said nothing about priests being descended from his tribe, Judah (7:14)—but by the "power of his indestructible life" (7:16). He is the only one who is "perfect forever" (7:28).

Those in deep suffering need God's mercy and forgiveness. All who take comfort in Yeshua the Messiah are restored day by day, "because he continually lives to intercede for them" (7:25).

CHAPTER NINE

I WILL MAKE A NEW COVENANT
HEBREWS 8:8

HEBREWS 8

At the core of Jewish discipleship was a very simple principle: retention through repetition. It was the responsibility of the student to attend carefully to every word of the rabbi. The rabbi would say something; the *talmid* (student) would repeat it to him, verbatim. Isaiah describes the ideal disciple:

> *The Sovereign* LORD *has given me the tongue of those who are taught, to know the word that sustains the weary. He wakens me morning by morning, wakens my ear to listen...and I have not been rebellious; I have not drawn back* (Isaiah 50:4–5) .

It is fitting that the one whom Scripture calls the Word (John 1:1) should desire the word of his father. Yeshua, as flesh and blood, needed that word. He studied it; it was his food (see John 4:34). In that word he discerned life's direction. Through that word he learned how to speak to "sustain the weary."

From a traditional Hebrew perspective, nothing is more important than study. It is the one "activity" that is most heartily pursued on the Sabbath. It is a source of rest and renewal for the soul.

When a Jewish child approaches the time of *bar* or *bat mitzvah*, he or she must study intensely to read from the *Torah* in the synagogue for the first time. The effort is a joy because, at thirteen, the child will come of age. Yet many Jewish children, especially in America, see their thirteenth year as a time when they may stop attending synagogue—as a time to express their "adulthood" by pursuing other interests.

Those who continue their studies may find it difficult to understand and apply Scriptures. Pertaining to Biblical studies, the saying, *shiv'im panim la-Torah*, "The Law has seventy faces," is a reminder that *Torah* can be interpreted many ways.

For those who undertake the study of more than five centuries of rabbinical thought—the *Talmud*—another maxim applies: *elu va-elu divrey Elohim khayim* ("both are the words of the living God"). This means that interpretations which are contrary to one another may both be acceptable.

Yeshua searched the Scriptures and listened to his father concerning them. He recognized his commitment not to be rebellious and not to draw back because of the horrible consequences: "I offered my back to those who beat me, my cheeks to those who pulled out my beard; I did not hide my face from mocking and spitting" (Isaiah 50:6).

Further, he knew himself to be the suffering servant of whom Isaiah prophesied: "He was pierced for our transgressions, he was crushed for our iniquities; the punishment that brought us peace was upon him, and by his wounds we are healed" (Isaiah 53:5).

Centuries before Isaiah, David spoke of the blessed happiness of him "whose transgression is forgiven, whose sin is covered, and unto whom iniquity is not imputed" (Psalm 32:1–2). Through the power of the spirit, Isaiah saw the promised Messiah who was "pierced for our transgressions," upon whom the Lord laid "the iniquity of us all," and who "bore the sin of many" (Isaiah 53:5, 6, 12).

The motto of the ancient rabbinical scholars, "search the Scriptures," was embraced with a diligent and painstaking thoroughness. Not a *yud*, the smallest Hebrew letter (the "jot" of Matthew 5:18) was overlooked. Yet for all of the efforts expended, secondary issues often obscured the most urgent matters in the 2,947 folio leaves comprising the *Talmud*.

Hebrews 8:1 wastes no time getting to the *ikar*, the heart of things: "The point of what we are saying is this." Having shown that the ceremonial law was "weak and useless" (7:18)—which includes the endless preoccupation with its precepts—the believer's attention is once again turned to him who speaks in our defense.

There is a Hebrew expression, *melamed zekhut*, which literally means "demonstrate innocence." What Yeshua the Messiah accomplished on his execution stake not only acquitted the believer but also established his innocence. Messiah's saving work is so comprehensive it is as if the forgiven sinner had never sinned.

In addition, there is a finality about the work of the Messiah. He is seated (8:1), signifying that his work is completed and perpetually effective for all who entrust themselves solely to him.

Everything that Israel had done in worship on earth—all the rituals and symbols—took place in a sphere which was a copy of reality. There was correspondence to the heavenly realities, but without substance. The priests were always busy, always in motion, standing, never finished—never at rest. All the symbols served to remind men of their separation from God; for where God is truly present, symbols are superfluous.

Of course, we are living in a world full of the evidence of sin, both within and around us. These may bring into question the reality of the new covenant which God's Messiah has "cut" with us.

It could, with some legitimacy, be argued that the time has not yet arrived for the elimination of all symbols. Yeshua, for example, appointed the use of the bread and wine of *Pesakh* (Passover), not to mention water, for such purposes. But God's completed work in Messiah would forever alter the way we approach God. The fruit of his labor is so remarkable that his accomplishments on behalf of his people are spelled out with great clarity and detail. But first, we need to understand the need for a "new covenant."

An incompleteness was evident in the old covenant, especially in the way the people of Israel related to God. Hebrew religion was characterized by a corporate relationship with God. It was the nation, an extended family, that was in covenant with the LORD. Israel, as a people, was God's son. The priests and prophets represented the nation before the LORD. Even when judgment was meted out, there was a collective dimension to it (Lamentations 5:7).

But Jeremiah's revelation did not end with that well-entrenched corporate concept of religion. He knew, as did the writer to the Hebrews, that there was something "wrong with that first covenant" (8:7). The fault was not in the agreement—it was "with the people" (8:8). His prophecy of a new and better covenant to a people about to be exiled is a message concerned with their healing. It is full of hope because the radical cure that is prescribed is directed right at the location of man's infection: his heart and mind.

What follows next is the longest quotation from the *Tenakh* to be found anywhere in *ha-B'rit ha-Khadashah* (the New Covenant):

The time is coming, declares the Lord, when I will make a new covenant with the house of Israel and with the house of Judah. It will not be like the covenant I made with their forefathers when I took them by the hand to lead them out of Egypt, because they did not remain faithful to my covenant, and I turned away from them, declares the Lord. This is the covenant I will make with the house of Israel after that time, says the Lord. I will put my laws in their minds and write them on their hearts. I will be their God, and they will be my people. No longer will a man teach his neighbor, or a man his brother, saying, "Know the Lord," because they will all know me, from the least of them to the greatest. For I will forgive their wickedness and remember their sins no more (8:8–12, quoting Jeremiah 31:31–34).

Although the rabbis spoke of the *yetzer hara*, the evil inclination, few took seriously Jeremiah's comment pronouncing the heart "incurably corrupt" (Jeremiah 17:9). Jewish thought also believed in the *yetzer hatov*, the good inclination. The *Talmudic* writers taught that Adam was created with both, although Rabbi Assi noted that the *yetzer hara* begins like a spider's thread but becomes like wagon ropes.

The best that natural man can produce is external religion. Although Jeremiah witnessed and gladly influenced the good reforms under king Josiah, the prophet could see that "Judah did not return [to the LORD] with all her heart" (Jeremiah 3:10).

What was needed was a wiping clean of man's filthy slate. A radical remedy is envisioned—personal knowledge of God. The verb that Jeremiah uses to "know" God is the same verb (*yada*) used to define the intimacy of Adam's relationship with Eve: "And Adam knew his wife; and she conceived" (Genesis 4:1).

The Hebrews are reminded that their intimate relationship with God is the result of his having totally forgiven their sins: "They will all know me...For I will forgive their wickedness and will remember their sins no more" (8:11–12).

God's "remembering" is always linked to action. God's "remembrance" of Cornelius (Acts 10:4) brought spiritual blessings to the man and his house. God's "remembering" Babylon will bring wrathful judgment (Revelation 16:19).

The author of Hebrews knew that the basis for God's new covenant is not essentially different from that of the covenant preceding it; but it is infinitely "better" (8:6). The old covenant and the new covenant do not differ regarding the shedding of blood as a prerequisite for reconciliation. The difference is to be found in the nature of what was sacrificed. The infinitely greater sacrifice of the Messiah accomplished what the first system could never do.

According to Jeremiah, God's will, to be truly effective, must be written "upon the heart," not on the memory, as the rabbis later emphasized. This was the internally inscribed covenant that formed the prophet's vision for the people of God.

It is said that Gamaliel II wept as he read Ezekiel, for he saw the extent of God's demands compared to his own inadequacies. Yet as Ezekiel dwelt among the exiled nation in Babylon, he offered his people hope as he expanded upon the promises of his older contemporary, Jeremiah. Ezekiel promised that God would replace his people's stony hearts with "hearts of flesh." He would place his spirit within them to enable them to obey him (Ezekiel 36:26–27). That will be God's gift to his people.

For the believer, God's *Torah* has been written not only on parchments but also on the core of his being. Life-giving grace has made it so—"Thanks be to God for his indescribable gift!" (2 Corinthians 9:15).

CHAPTER TEN

HOW MUCH MORE, THEN, WILL THE BLOOD OF THE MESSIAH... CLEANSE OUR CONSCIENCES

HEBREWS 9:14

HEBREWS 9

From early times, every Jewish community has had a *mikveh*, a pool for ceremonial cleansing. Immersion in its waters is never more important than just prior to *Yom Kippur*. Being clean before God is the concern of every true worshipper.

The *Tenakh* abounds with examples revealing man's defilement. Our first parents knew the shame of defilement when they transgressed God's command (Genesis 3:10).

Aaron and his sons had to wash their hands and feet whenever they drew near to worship God; failure to comply with this lasting ordinance would result in death (Exodus 30:17–21).

Concern for purity extended to one's livestock; God would not receive a sacrificial offering that was blemished or defective in any way (Exodus 12:5). And only a select group from among the twelve tribes—the *kohanim* (priests)—could bring those acceptable offerings to the LORD. The High Priest alone was permitted to enter the holiest place beyond the tabernacle's inner veil, once a year on *Yom Kippur*, the Day of Atonement (9:7).

There was cleansing, but not thorough cleansing. The writer reminds the Hebrews that under the old system the best they could hope for was a limited *kedushah* (sanctity), for the blood of goats and bulls could never accomplish deep internal cleansing (9:9).

In addition, there was an extraordinary form of ritual cleansing. Moses was given a regulation which became an increasingly significant part of Israel's worship experience. Numbers 19 describes the ceremony: a perfect red heifer, which had never been yoked, was slaughtered outside the camp of Israel. After sprinkling its blood seven times in front of the tabernacle, the animal was consumed by fire and its ashes stored for mixing with water.

Water of cleansing (*me niddah*) containing those ashes was applied to those who had been defiled as a result of coming near to or touching a dead body. The High Priest was no exception; he was sprinkled with the purifying waters twice during the week immediately preceding *Yom Kippur*, just in case he unknowingly became ceremonially defiled.

After the destruction of the Temple and its sacrificial altar in 70 C.E., the water for these washings could no longer be made. According to the *Mishnah*, the last priest to kill a red heifer was the High Priest *Ishmael ben Phabi* ten years before the razing of Jerusalem. (Stored ashes could last for a decade.)

The Samaritans, who viewed Jerusalem's Temple indifferently, continued their slaying of red heifers until the fourteenth century, using those ashes for generations afterwards. Maimonides (a twelfth century scholar) believed that the red heifer ritual would be resumed with the coming of the Messiah.

The problem is that this, like so many of Israel's rituals, dealt with the externals of religion. The sometimes elaborate and impressive procedures "were not able to cleanse the conscience of the worshipper" (9:9). They could not touch the inner defilement which prevented fellowship with the Holy One of Israel. Our inward sense of guilt and estrangement required "better sacrifices than these" (9:23).

The society at Qumran, where the Dead Sea Scrolls were found, warned that no amount of cleansing could help a soul who wasn't truly penitent. But, as the penitent thief found, real purification could be received as a gift from him who came to "sprinkle many nations" (Isaiah 52:15).

Penitence accompanied by ritualistic cleansing cannot bring peace to a sin-ravaged soul. No amount of religious activity will suffice; its proliferation only heightens our awareness that we are not fully reconciled to God.

As a boy, I congratulated myself for fasting during part of *Yom Kippur*. I loved food too much to endure the entire day, but thought that my abstinence made God especially pleased. Perhaps it did. But my childhood hopes eventually gave way to the stark reality that I was spiritually hungry. The absence of food was only part of my emptiness.

Moses said that God caused us to hunger in the desert so that we would gratefully receive his provision of *manna* and rely solely upon the word of his covenant (Deuteronomy 8:3). But history revealed Israel's predisposition to rely on other resources, drinking from the "broken cisterns" we devised. "Utterly faithless!" is Jeremiah's indictment (Jeremiah 2:13; 5:11).

Israel's prophets tried to *hakrev* (bring closer) the people to their God, but without success. Isaiah's evaluation of the people's failure gets right to the point: "All of our righteous acts are as filthy rags" (Isaiah 64:6).

In western culture a child is usually reproved for unacceptable behavior with words like: "That's wrong!" or "That's bad!" In the Middle East, a child is told, "That is shameful!"

All the ceremonial laws which the Hebrews were no longer obligated to obey because of the Messiah's sacrifice were a reminder of man's defiled, shameful condition before him who is "*kadosh, kadosh, kadosh*," "holy, holy, holy" (Isaiah 6:3). The fiery *seraphim*, though sinless creatures, covered themselves in his presence (Isaiah 6:2). Only the worst sort of arrogance could suppose that humanity may naturally stand before God guiltless and unashamed.

Two of Messiah's messengers, Peter and Paul, said that the one who trusts in him "will not be ashamed"—*lo yevosh*—(Romans 9:33; 1 Peter

2:6). The Hebrews needed never to fear that their trust in "the Mediator of the New Covenant" (9:15) would prove to be ill-founded. The unbelieving Jewish community had become like those whose taunting is recorded in the Psalms, previously spoken against Yeshua: "He trusts in God; let God deliver him, since he delights in him" (Psalm 22:8).

God would vindicate his people's biblically-informed trust in the Messiah, a reliance beautifully summed up generations ago by Edward Mote: "Dressed in his righteousness alone, faultless to stand before the throne."

Messiah did away with sin through the sacrifice of himself (9:26). But only the irrepressible grace of God can bring individuals to see both their foul character and his cleansing provision.

The utter finality of Messiah's sacrifice is a recurring theme in Hebrews. In chapter nine the author uses strong words conveying the idea, "once for all" (9:12, 26, 28). He also plays on a word corresponding to the Hebrew, *b'rit* , which can mean either "covenant" or "will." In verse 15, the word's former sense is indicated. But in verse 16, the etymology is apparently stretched to embrace the latter: "In the case of a will, it is necessary to prove the death of the one who made it, because a will is in force only when somebody has died. The will never takes effect while the one who made it is living" (9:16–17).

Both verses speak of an inheritance which Messiah gives his people. Covenantally, his death brought all of God's rich promises. Although it is true that "Abraham received what was promised" (6:15), his hope looked forward to the time of the Messiah: he saw Yeshua's day and rejoiced (John 8:56).

Our defilement is the result of our fallen nature. The inner filthiness that separates us from the Holy One and his "promised eternal inheritance" (9:15) cannot be washed away by any human cleanser. Only "by [Yeshua's] own blood" (9:12) are we made clean in his sight, becoming heirs of that life which we will enjoy forever in the presence of God.

The notion of an inheritance turns the writer's thoughts to a well-known type of legal document. The last will and testament of a Jewish father, known as *tsava'ah*, traditionally a patriarch's final means to communicate moral responsibility to the surviving family. Material acquisitions were of little value if he who possessed them failed to live a godly life.

Yeshua tells the story of a young man who asked for his inheritance while his father was still alive—a most reprehensible request. Still, it did not sever the son from his father's gracious love (Luke 15:11–32). A careful reading of the text shows that the development of the young man's moral character—his repentance actually began in his stomach—would have to follow an experience of the father's grace.

Grace is the foundation for all righteousness, legal and experiential. The cleansing of the conscience—a divinely initiated and implemented work—opens the way for us "to serve the living God" (9:14). Of course, any analogy based on a last will cannot be pressed too far. After all, the maker of the will—our Testator—not only died but also rose again.

Because "the living God" is with us, it is unconscionable to return to those former ways which have now become "obsolete" (8:13). What a relief to be set free from the unending regulations which governed Jewish life from dawn till dark. The rituals often bound my people more to earth than to heaven.

When the author tells the believers that they have been "redeemed" (9:15), he uses a slave-market term (see NIV's "set free") that would have struck a responsive chord. They have been released from sin's oppressive tyranny; they have been liberated to serve God in the spirit, not in ritual. As they reflect on all that they have received from the Lord, no legacy can equal their priceless freedom in the Messiah.

But the community also needed reassurance that their faith in God's work was sufficient for salvation without any added works of the Law. The writer confirms that the Messiah truly "died as a ransom to set them free from the sins committed under the first covenant" (9:15).

The eternal inheritance given them was also an encouragement to withstand the abuse of their opposition. They were in the midst of great *tsarot* (troubles). Their earthly belongings as well as their very lives were in constant jeopardy. But they are offered more than a future relief from their woes. Messiah, who would one day "appear a second time...to bring salvation" (9:28) had already enabled them to "taste the goodness of the word of God and the powers of the coming age" (6:5).

Among the choicest of blessings one Jewish man gives to another is that he may be called a *ben-khayil*, a son of valor. If the person to be blessed is a woman, she may be called *eshet khayil*, a woman of valor, what the woman described in Proverbs 31 is called. The psalmist spoke of God's people going *me-khayil el khayil*, from strength to strength, along life's pilgrimage (Psalm 84:7). He sees their pathway through a sorrowful valley (*bakha*), yet proclaims, "O LORD Almighty, blessed is the man who trusts in you" (Psalm 84:12).

In Messiah, the believers would find strength to meet all the vast array of life's obstacles and live to serve their savior with his full acceptance. No matter what the circumstances, he is "an ever-present help in times of troubles [*tsarot*]" (Psalm 46:1).

CHAPTER ELEVEN

THE LAW IS ONLY A SHADOW
HEBREWS 10:1

HEBREWS 10:1–18

My people have often thought of themselves as having a love relationship with the *Torah*. Among the greatest honors a synagogue may bestow upon one of its own is to designate a person the *Khatan Torah* (Bridegroom of the *Torah*) or the *Khatan B'reshit* (Bridegroom of Genesis). These titles are bestowed with all the pageantry associated with a real wedding. This is done in honor of being called forward to read the opening or closing lines of the *Torah* during *Simchat Torah*, the festival of rejoicing over the *Torah*.

It is not uncommon to hear the rabbis speak of the Law as the marriage contract which binds *Adonai*, Israel's husband, to his Hebrew bride. God never breaks his contract (since he is totally faithful), yet what of humanity?

The *Kabbalah*, Israel's secret book of mysticism from the Middle Ages, was once read by many. Its esoteric writings are concerned with attaining intimate knowledge of the Almighty, though its thoughts are obviously human. The title *Kabbalah* means "tradition"—rather than revelation.

This mystical book defines a principle which has governed Jewish orthodoxy since the time of Moses: *kol ha-mosif gorea* (to add is to detract). In reference to Holy Scripture, you dare not enlarge on that which God has communicated. The command is found in Deuteronomy 4:2 and in Revelation's final warnings (Revelation 22:18). It is an instruction that many, in their zeal to find redemption through the Law, have disregarded.

The author or authors of *Kabbalah* held that the Law is the binding link between God and his people: "Know thou that the 613 Precepts of the Law form a compact with the Holy One—blessed be he!—and with Israel" (*Kitzur Sh'lu*, p.2, col. 2). The *Kabbalist* goes on to state that "No one is perfect unless he has thoroughly observed all the 613 precepts."

But then the question is raised: "If this be so, who is he and where is he that has observed all the 613 precepts? For even the lord of the prophets, Moses our Rabbi—peace be on him!—had not observed them all." The *Kabbalist* is forced to reach an accommodation: "Therefore every Israelite is bound to observe only such of the 613 precepts as are possible for him; and such as he has not observed, in consequence of hindrances arising from unpreventable causes, will be reckoned to him as if actually performed." Presumably, at some point, the religiously observant Jew will have to do an extensive *kheshbon ha-nefesh* (soul-searching) in an attempt to distinguish between legitimate and illegitimate hindrances with the hope of assuaging his guilty conscience.

Yet reaching a point where people "would no longer have felt guilty for their sins" (10:2) could only be achieved by accepting the individual's word over God's word. We are forever clinging to man's lesser standard lest the achievement of perfection remain an elusive dream to us.

How we feel about ourselves seems to be more important than God's objective, honest evaluation of us. Yet the constant religious activity of priests and populace underscored the reality that no amount of human-centered piety could "make perfect those who draw near to worship" (10:1).

Perfection for the writer to the Hebrews is the ability to have ongoing intimacy with God without having constantly to remove the barrier of newly accumulated sin. He refers to Jeremiah's prophesied covenant to refresh the Jewish believers with the thought that their continual access to God has been made possible by grace alone (10:16–17).

Our heavenly father is the one who sprinkles our hearts and cleanses our consciences (10:22). As Jeremiah's younger contemporary, Ezekiel, so forcefully put it: "I will sprinkle clean water on you...I will give you a new heart...I will put my spirit in you" (Ezekiel 36:25–27).

The provision of God for our intimate communion with him is not, then, a "different" covenant. It contains a full measure of the grace which was offered long before. Those who had discerned its true substance knew the crippling power of sin and gratefully responded to the prophet Hosea's call by saying: "Forgive all our sins and receive us graciously" (Hosea 14:2).

The New Covenant was responsive to the Law, but not based upon it. No legal contract bound Israel, God's faithless bride, to her beloved spouse.

Jeremiah dwells on the multidimensional character of God's covenant love early in chapter 31: "I have loved you with an everlasting love (*ahavah*); therefore I have continued to love (*khesed*) you" (Jeremiah 31:3). The first term used by the prophet is a general term for love; it is the second term, however, which reveals God's loving-kindness and unflinching commitment to his bride. *Khesed* is a deep, persistent love which provides whatever is necessary for the sake of the loved one.

Even when the beloved is wayward, like Hosea's wife, Gomer, such love cries out, "How can I give you up?" (Hosea 11:8). In its extraordinary persistence, the voice of love says of an unworthy people, "I will heal their waywardness and love them freely" (Hosea 14:4). This is because the eternal covenant with Israel is not a code of law but, rather, "the faithful mercies of David" (Isaiah 55:3).

When Israel's exiles hung their harps on the distant poplars of Babylon, the psalmist remembered that bond eternally shaped by the *khesed* of God: *Im eshkakhekh Yerushalayim tishkakh yemini*, "If I forget you, O Jerusalem, may my right hand forget its skill" (Psalm 137:5).

Yet the righteous anger which was justly issued from a holy God and which was "turned away from them" (Hosea 14:4) did not evaporate into thin air. The wrath of God against sin was absorbed in its incalculable fullness by him who said, "Sacrifice and offering you did not desire, but a body you prepared for me" (10:5).

Some six centuries before, God told Jeremiah to "take a scroll and write on it all the words I have spoken to you concerning Israel" (Jeremiah 36:2). The prophet saw an oppressed people in need of a strong redeemer (Jeremiah 50:33–34). The heart of his message concerned their liberation from their cruel, unrelenting captors. The scroll also contained the Law and the prophet's witness to its innumerable violations by a rebellious people (see Numbers 9:24), a people in need of healing, as Isaiah had said, "from the foot's sole to the top of the head" (Isaiah 1:6).

Within the Bible's message of physical deliverance, we see the prophetic anticipation of radical measures to restore the people of God. The corporate religious expression finds a glorious, individual component as God's covenant is "written upon the individual's heart." No deeper inscription can be made than that which is written upon the *lev*, the heart.

In order to have radical results, an equally radical work was required, the coming of the one anticipated in the scroll of Jeremiah and all the prophetic writings. His death would accomplish man's healing transformation. Before his incarnation, no one except the prophets could understand the full extent of God's love.

While Jeremiah's thoughts about the New Covenant were informed by Psalm 40:6–8, the writer to the Hebrews sees Messiah as the fulfillment of Jeremiah's words (Jeremiah 36:2–3):

Sacrifice and offering you did not desire, but a body you prepared for me;
With burnt offerings and sin offerings you were not pleased.
Then I said, Here I am—it is written about me in the scroll—
I have come to do your will, O God. (10:5–7)

Hebraists will note that the quoted words are not found in the Hebrew text of Psalm 40:6–8. They are taken from the Greek Old Testament (the Septuagint). Yet the Hebrew Masoretic reading, "ears have you dug for me" (in lieu of "a body you have prepared for me") conveys the same message: a prepared readiness to do the will of God. The "digging" of the ear finds a ready link with one of the great servant song prophecies of Isaiah: "The Sovereign LORD...wakens me morning by morning, wakens my ear to listen" (Psalm 50:4).

The savior of humanity would find that his dedication would also necessitate the offering up of his back to beatings, his cheeks to those who pulled out his beard, and his face to mocking and spitting (Isaiah 50:6). The attentive submission to his father's words would lead to "pouring out his life unto death" and even being "numbered (identified) with the transgressors" (Isaiah 53:12).

After the atoning work of Yeshua, the sacrifices of the past, though ordained by God, no longer pleased him (10:6). The Messiah's perfect obedience unto death rendered their value null and void. They had accomplished their purpose of testifying eloquently to the coming one. His sanctifying work had taken place "once for all" (10:10) and produced an inward cleansing that gives his people "confidence to enter the Most Holy Place" (10:19).

Having begun this chapter with a reference to marriage, I am reminded of the very ancient tradition of the *khupah*. This is the wedding canopy under which Jewish couples exchange their matrimonial vows. The beautiful cloth, held up on four poles, symbolizes the bride's and groom's future home and dwelling with God.

From Israel's earliest times, the sealing of the marriage covenant also included the transfer of gifts. In the ancient Near East, the groom's gift was considered to be actually an extension of himself and indirectly established his authority over his bride. In Israel, this was also a reminder that God had given himself to his bride. It is always God who has provided even the nation's most basic needs—"the grain, the wine and oil" (Hosea 2:8).

Our righteous heavenly husband has said, "I will betroth you to me forever; I will betroth you in righteousness and justice...in *khesed.*" Best of all, as a wife intimately "knows" her husband, God's people will "know the LORD" (Hosea 2:19–20).

In the closing chapters of Old Testament history, God declared through his prophet Malachi, "I hate divorce" (Malachi 2:16). God is truly married to his people for "better or for worse." He is the Sovereign LORD whose gift of the Holy Spirit will bring all of his good purposes to fruition—in us and for us.

Few truths alleviate a troubled soul's discouragement more than the realization that Yeshua's sacrifice has forever made us perfect in God's sight (10:14). This is confirmed in the closing chapters of the New Testament—and the final chapter of life on this earth—where God's "bride" is given "fine linen, bright and clean" (Revelation 19:8).

Through faith in Yeshua the Messiah, we will one day join that small group of Jewish believers who first read this letter, and together we will reflect that divine purity before all principalities and powers—beyond any doubt.

CHAPTER TWELVE

LET US DRAW NEAR TO GOD
HEBREWS 10:22

HEBREWS 10:19–39

Messiah's finished work enables us to "draw near" to God. For the Jewish believers to whom the letter was written, "let us draw near" called to mind the expression inviting worshippers to approach the Temple following the offering of a sacrifice.

Now, though, they could approach with confidence because of their *kohen gadol* ("great High Priest"—10:21). His sacrifice had, in effect, ripped in two ("from top to bottom"—see Matthew 27:51) the massive curtain which separated them from the Holy of Holies.

The *Torah* required the officiating priests to wash themselves whenever they approached God in service (Exodus 30:19–21). But external washings could not cleanse the heart; only Yeshua could accomplish that internal transformation: "He saved us through the washing of rebirth and renewal by the Holy Spirit, whom he poured out on us generously" (Titus 3:5).

A fundamental part of the New Covenant's blessing was described by Ezekiel: "I will sprinkle clean water on you...I will cleanse you from all your impurities" (Ezekiel 36:25). God's redemptive work not only involved inward cleansing but also the giving of his *Ruakh* (Spirit) to his people: "I will put my spirit in you" (Ezekiel 36:27).

Ruakh is used in Scripture in a variety of ways. It often means wind, but has other meanings, as well. The *Ruakh* of God is mentioned in the creation narrative: "In the beginning *Ruakh Elohim* [the Spirit of God] was hovering over the waters" (Genesis 1:1).

Some use the word loosely to describe a kind of spirit which occasionally comes over people, especially at a lively *simkhah* (celebration). *Ruakh* also refers to *ha-Ruakh ha-Kodesh* (the Holy Spirit).

The term *ha-Ruakh ha-Kodesh* has been used to describe rare individuals who show a high degree of godliness. Furthermore, in Jewish thought no distinct person was linked to "the Holy Spirit." Its usage usually amounted to ascribing spirituality to someone.

Yet, Yeshua began his public ministry by reading Isaiah's witness to the Spirit's anointing: "The *Ruakh* of the Lord God is upon me" (Isaiah 61:1). The Master also stated that "unless one is born of water and the Spirit, he cannot enter the kingdom of God" (John 3:5). Later in Hebrews 10, the believer is warned not to insult "the Spirit of grace" (10:29), who has applied the Messiah's sanctifying work to his heart.

One way of insulting the Holy Spirit is to act as though he were not present to accomplish God's purposes in one's life. If one denies his influence and disregards his life-changing power, then he is treating "as an unholy thing the blood of the covenant" (10:29).

A high rabbinic ideal is found in a *Talmudic* expression "to expound properly and practice properly." This means that an individual lives in accordance with the truth he has spoken. For those who took this maxim seriously, the New Covenant's testimony concerning *ha-Ruakh ha-Kodesh* would have been no lifeless, academic doctrine.

The Spirit not only "testifies to us" concerning God's salvation (10:15) but also brings us into that "living way" (10:20) which is nothing less than personal contact with God (John 14:6). Without the Spirit, real prayer is impossible even though we are not always conscious of his direct intercession (see Romans 8:26–27).

Few believers realize how indebted they are to the Holy Spirit. But their acceptance of Yeshua, the one "numbered with transgressors" and bearer of God's redeeming, life-changing love would never have been accepted without the Spirit's irresistible influence. This was especially true for these Hellenized Jews.

The *Talmud* uses a graphic metaphor to describe someone whose religious activity is nothing more than hypocrisy: *tovel ve-sherets b'yado* ("immersed in water with a reptile in his hand"). The image is of one who goes through immersion for the sake of purification—from such impure objects as dead reptiles—and makes a travesty of these actions.

Hebrews urges the believers to approach God "with a true heart" (10:22). The heart produced by the Holy Spirit is characterized by a sincere, single-mindedness inasmuch as it has been cleansed from all unrighteousness. There is no place for hypocrisy in the prayer life of anyone whom God has declared clean.

Many laws of *Torah* remind the child of God to be singularly devoted to the God whose covenant in blood "has sanctified him" (10:29). For example, the Jew is forbidden to mix wool and linen in one garment; such a mixture is described as *sha'atnez* (Deuteronomy 22:11).

Similar reminders of one's obligation to obey God are everywhere in Judaism. As one enters a Jewish home, a small container (*mezuzah*) is attached to the doorway. Inside are tiny parchments of Scripture. Its placement is in response to the command to write God's Word "on the doorframes of your houses" (Deuteronomy 11:20). The same passage commands us to tie God's words "as symbols on your hands and bind them on your foreheads" (Deuteronomy 11:18). Israel responded literally with what are called *tefillin*—phylacteries— small boxes containing Bible verses, strapped to the left arm and forehead, worn regularly during prayer.

The large prayer shawl (*tallit*), with its many hanging threads serves as a reminder of the *Torah's* numerous commandments. Wrapped in its wide, massive cloth, the worshipper may sense God's nearness, even his enveloping love.

Again and again the Jewish worshippers respond to law upon law, precept upon precept. The Law confronts them when they are resting or rising, sitting or walking (Deuteronomy 11:19). Why so many? Why did they seem nearly endless? To cause him never to lose sight of the fact that he belonged to God and was responsible to his creator and redeemer.

The writer to the Hebrews reminded them that they belonged to God and were responsible to him. They were to become sensitive and not resist the Spirit's gracious influence (10:29). They were a people who desperately needed his help as they faced being "publicly exposed to insult and persecution," and having their property confiscated (10:33–34).

It was never God's intention that the believer should have to make a spiritual go of it on his own. The Holy Spirit revealed two provisions for spiritual well-being. First, to not give up meeting together and second, to encourage one another.

One may survive alone, but one cannot prosper, spiritually, in isolation. A *Talmudic* saying, "All Jews are responsible for one another," spoke to this. There were those in the community of believers who were disregarding their need for fellowship, making themselves vulnerable to forces that could undermine and weaken them spiritually.

Earlier, the letter compared the believers to Israel in the wilderness (3:7–4:13). This is no forced comparison. Like Israel of old, the believers were on an extended journey to a marvelous destination. In *Talmudic* terms, this world (*ha-olam ha-zeh*) is a passageway to the next world (*ha-olam ha-ba*). But there are dangers along the way. The believers dared not confront them on their own. So the warning is given: "Do not stay away from the meetings of fellow believers; you need their fellowship." (10:25) As they made their journey in faith together, like Israel in the desert, even a wild wilderness may become a place of peace.

As a new believer, I desperately needed the support of others who loved the Messiah. After my experience of the new birth, I thought I was the only Jew in New York—perhaps in the world—who believed in Yeshua. Those early months lacked a "fullness of faith" (10:22), largely because my experience of the Messiah was being lived in isolation.

Finally, the Lord sent a concerned pastor into the studios at CBS where I was employed. As a result, I became part of a community. We all had our flaws, but we shared the love of Messiah, who had made us holy through his "one sacrifice for sins" (10:12). My friends had gathered together because they had come to understand their continual need of one another. They strengthened each other as they confronted life's struggles. And with them I too found the strength to carry on.

The second provision of God flows from the first. Meeting regularly with one another gives encouragement and inspiration to do God's good work in this world.

It's hard to know precisely the point it began, but traditionally Jews do not hold a prayer meeting without a *minyan* (quorum of ten). Apparently, since Abraham begged God to spare Sodom and Gomorrah if only ten righteous people could be found there, a precedent was established that ten Jewish male adults must gather together before prayer may commence.

Lewis Glinert (Hebrew scholar at the University of London), in his *Joys of Hebrew* (p. 160), tells of a group who wanted to say *m'nakhot* (afternoon prayers) but they were only nine in number. The rabbi peered out of the synagogue window only to see a well-known atheist coming out of a pork store. "Quick, call him to make the *minyan!*" the rabbi shouted to the synagogue's usher. "What, him?!" said the usher. "An atheist?!" "Why not?" said the rabbi. "We're nine, so we're only short of one zero."

Whether there are ten or only two (note Matthew 18:19–20), nothing is more important than God's people getting together for prayer and fellowship. Nothing exceeds the value of this *akhdut* (togetherness). Early in the letter, all believers are called "holy brothers" (3:1). The act of God that separated them from the unbelievers also created a family bond between them. We are never more secure in the Messiah than when that shared faith leads us to "daily encourage one another" (3:13).

The closing section of Hebrews 10 is a challenge to patient endurance. But it goes a step further and calls us to something beyond static resignation. The author's quote from Habakkuk is well chosen. This prophet was given to understand that Israel would soon be devastated by the ruthless Babylonians (Habakkuk 1:6). The approaching violence caused Habakkuk's heart to pound, his lips to quiver, his legs to tremble (Habakkuk 3:16). His final prophetic word informed all that would hear him that he would yet "rejoice in the LORD" and "be joyful in God my savior" (Habakkuk 3:18). Habakkuk knew, as did the author of Hebrews, that the current indignities and terrors would not prevail.

God gave his word that Yeshua, who had dwelt among them, died, and rose again, "will appear a second time, not to bear sin, but to bring salvation to those who are waiting for him" (9:28). In that day we will receive our "better and lasting possessions" (10:34).

At present we, like the Hebrew believers of old, are engaged in a "great contest" (10:32). We will emerge triumphantly by standing firm, which is a way of saying "live by faith" (10:38). By God's grace and through the fellowship of the Holy One and one another, we will be part of that vast company.

CHAPTER THIRTEEN

NOW FAITH IS BEING SURE OF WHAT WE HOPE FOR AND CERTAIN OF WHAT WE DO NOT SEE
HEBREWS 11:1

HEBREWS 11

Hebrew has more than one word that is translated "miracle" or "sign." *Ot* occurs in the Exodus narrative where God commands Moses to use his staff to do "signs" in Egypt (Exodus 4:17). The word also appears earlier when Moses is hesitant to be God's man before Pharaoh. In response to his doubts, God offers him an unusual *ot*: "And this will be the sign [*ot*] to you that it is I who have sent you: When you have brought the people out of Egypt, you will worship God on this mountain" (Exodus 3:12).

Israel has long identified different types of signs (using the word *nes*, meaning "miracle"). There are "big ones" such as the birth of Isaac to Sarah in her ninetieth year, the plagues in Egypt, the parting of the sea. And there are "little ones" given miraculous status by modern Israelis, such as their victory in the Six-Day War and recent peace accords.

Talmudic wisdom doubts that those actually benefiting from God's *nissim* (miracles) are truly aware of them. As we follow Israel in the desert the truth of this axiom becomes evident. It's clear that the acts of God on her behalf are soon regarded as commonplace: the deliverance miracles, the *manna*, the shoes that didn't wear out, all seem to have little effect on the people led by Moses, whom he calls "stiff-necked" (Exodus 33:3). When you come right down to it, there is precious little separating the Israelites then from all other generations. Even Yeshua's disciples had "little faith" (Luke 12:28).

The word *nes* begins to show its complexities in a Biblical passage that follows Israel's liberation from Egypt. During the battle with the Amalekites at *Rephidim*, Moses, with uplifted hands, saw his fighting people emerge triumphant. He built an altar there, calling it *Adonai-nissi* (Exodus 17:15). Here *nes* is in the possessive form. Moses is not saying, "The LORD is my miracle" but, "The Lord is my banner." It is hardly accidental that the latter expression is connected with the word ordinarily meaning miracle. Believers know that God is the standard around whom we rally. He is also our miracle-working savior.

Still another, even more curious, usage of *nes* draws our attention. The setting is still the wilderness, but this time we observe one of the most horrible incidents in Israel's history. Multitudes of venomous snakes attacked the people (Numbers 21:6). In response to Moses' intercession for the dying Israelites, The LORD said, "Make a snake and put it on a *nes*; anyone who is bitten can look at it and live" (Numbers 21:8). The image of a brass serpent—a raised standard—was God's means of deliverance.

I have no doubt that there were those among the bitten people who thought the idea of gazing up at a pole with a crudely fashioned snake-like object upon it may have seemed ridiculous. Those people died. Those who looked and lived were sure of what they hoped for (11:1). They had faith.

Just prior to the glorious statement in John's Gospel that tells how much God loved the world, Yeshua said to Nicodemus, a member of the Jewish ruling council, "Just as Moses lifted up the snake in the desert, so the Son of Man must be lifted up, that everyone who believes in him may have eternal life" (John 3:14–15). There is no question concerning the analogy. An uplifted form had been invested with the power to heal. All that was required was faith in the raised provision. It appears that Nicodemus eventually got the message.

There is still one more word used to indicate the miraculous which, in modern Hebrew, is the equivalent of *nes*. That word is *pele*. Students of Messianic prophecy recognize *pele* in Isaiah's description of Israel's wonder-full king (Isaiah 9:6).

From Isaiah's vantage point, the wonderful nature of Messiah is inextricably linked to his role as counselor. Just as Hebrews 11:1 tells us that faith means putting our full confidence in what we hope for, we must trust in Yeshua's words. Yeshua the Messiah, the wonderful counselor, said, "Take my yoke upon you and learn from me." When we respond in this way, according to Messiah, "You will find rest for your souls" (Matthew 11:29).

Yeshua is not simply trying to induce us into a rabbi-disciple relationship. He is calling us to cleave to him fully. It is not only the word from the Messiah that saves us, but also the word about the Messiah which, when believed, alters our eternal destiny. Biblical faith is more than simple belief. It involves a genuine relationship with Yeshua who is uplifted before us.

Messianic Jews recognized that their belief in a crucified Messiah ran so contrary to Jewish expectations that only a miracle-working God—who makes faith a gift, as Paul says (Ephesians 2:8)—could have brought them to believe in Yeshua. For a devout Jewish person to embrace such a new concept of their Davidic King-Messiah, before whom it was prophesied that all nations were to bow in obeisance (Psalm 2:8–9), is a miracle of the highest order.

Those who "know the Lord" get to that place supernaturally, because another wonderful counselor, the Holy Spirit, is at work in their lives. Of this counselor Yeshua said, "He will convict the world of guilt in regard to sin" (John 16:8). Grace, which provides faith, brings us to see our need for the savior. Above all, it leads us to desire a personal intimacy with him.

Faith has an objective basis. We believe in the miraculous historical events of Yeshua's life recorded that give rise to faith (John 20:30–31). But we have not trusted in Yeshua only as a result of some dispassionate intellectual dissection of these records. In the final analysis, I do not believe that anyone can just use the evidence to convince themselves of Yeshua's Messiahship and all that entails, anymore than an individual can come to the Messiah "unless," as Yeshua said, "the Father who sent me draws him" (John 6:44).

The reason for this is our terrible lostness. Jeremiah's sweeping evaluation of our wretched hearts (Jeremiah 17:9) is repeated in the New Testament's damning indictment of our collective depravity: "There is no one who understands, no one who seeks God. All have turned away" (Romans 3:11–12).

Faith, though it is works with reason, is a higher faculty than reason. Its source is God. Lefevre d'Etaples says it so well:

Reason does not attain to faith, but grace, which is superior to reason, provides it...He who is unwilling to leave behind the possibility of his own reason encloses himself in a dark and confining prison where the sun of grace does not shine and life-giving faith is not found.

Faith has supernatural underpinnings from first to last. It is not, as some philosopher-theologians have defined it, "a leap in the dark," although we cannot prove the existence of the realities in which we hope. For now, they remain unseen. But because we are stewards of God's gift—that faith which has come to us from beyond ourselves—we should not be surprised if we are often compelled to cry out, "Lord, I believe; help thou my unbelief."

Noah, Abraham, Sarah, and the others of Hebrews 11, some of them "little" people in the world's estimation, all made it clear that they were seeking a homeland. They were "aliens and strangers on earth" (11:13). Although the inner process which led each one to faith was shrouded in mystery, we know the way with which God brought them to faith. It is stated clearly in Romans 10:17: "Faith comes from hearing the message, and the message is heard through the word of Messiah."

In Hebrew, the word *davar* means both word and deed. This is because the word which comes from God, by virtue of its source, is powerful. God's word doesn't just say something; it accomplishes something and makes great things happen: "The world was created by the word of God" (11:3).

Our God, whose creation came into being through the direct participation of the living Word (John 1:3) has, through that Word, re-created us: "For it is the same God who said, 'Let light shine out of darkness,' who has shone in our hearts to give us the light of the knowledge of the glory of God in the face of Messiah" (2 Corinthians 4:6). The Messiah is the agent of both the first creation and of our re-creation as well. We have been born anew "through the living and abiding Word of God" (1 Peter 1:23).

At the outset of this chapter we considered how extraordinary it is to be part of a worshipping people. We have come to understand that the regenerating force which enables us to know Messiah is like the mighty power which raised him from the dead (Ephesians 1:18–20). Our heavenly Father, who has produced this change within us, will never allow us to get too comfortable in this present world. He has called us to something far higher, far better.

Synagogues practice the *aliyah* (ascent), meaning to go up to the platform to read from the *Torah*. During a regular Sabbath service it is likely that several men will be invited to "make an *aliyah*." But the expression does double duty in that it also refers to those Jews who immigrate to their national homeland, who "make *aliyah*" to the place of their spiritual roots.

Jewish expositors have consistently regarded their ancient forebears as those who "ascended from Egypt to Israel." All this serves to remind us that our encampment here is temporary. Even now, through faith, we learn our higher dwelling place is not as remote as our senses may indicate. The Letter to the Hebrews says to all believers: "You have come to Mount Zion, to the heavenly Jerusalem, the city of the living God."

And to show the reader that he now, by faith, actually has a foot in heaven, the writer adds, "You have come to thousands upon thousands of angels in joyful assembly" (12:22).

Everything on earth is decaying or breaking around us daily. Even in moments of joy we are reminded of our agonies. Sometimes it is the past that haunts us. The contemporary poet, *Yehuda Amichai*, observed, "Most people of our time have the face of Lot's wife turned toward the *Shoah* (Nazi Holocaust) and yet they are always escaping."

At Jewish weddings, the groom crushes a glass under his foot in remembrance of the Temple's destruction. In Jerusalem it is customary to restrict the wedding music to just one lone drum. But as my friend Rachmiel Frydland—a Jewish believer now in glory—used to say, "In the evening, weeping may lodge with us but in the morning there will be *rinnah*, joyous shouting!" (Psalm 30:5).

You can not judge God's calling or purposes by the presence of painful adversities. The Hebrews are reminded that many of God's people endured severe physical and emotional afflictions, including cruel mocking and torturous executions (11:36–37). But, by the grace which sustains faith, their confidence remained in God. For us, too, despite difficult circumstances that demand all our attention, God and his treasures must remain unseen until the day we die. At best "we see through a glass darkly." But by grace our hearts will delight in the promises of that future reality, although only the first fruits are available to us.

Regardless of what sufferings we may endure, they pale by comparison to those of the Messiah. He was intimately "acquainted with grief...was wounded for our transgressions ...was crushed for our iniquities." He was the one upon whom was laid "the iniquity of us all" (Isaiah 53).

We take heart as we remember what he suffered for our sakes. The Master has called us to be like him, even in embracing hardship (Matthew 10:25). His promise is true that, with endurance, we will forever "reign with him" (2 Timothy 2:12).

CHAPTER FOURTEEN

BUT YOU HAVE COME TO THE CITY OF THE LIVING GOD
HEBREWS 12:22

HEBREWS 12

The glory and supremacy of the Messiah is the great theme of Hebrews. The Hebrew believers in Messiah were doubtless told by an antagonistic community that they had turned their backs on God. They were probably taunted for having foolishly forsaken Jerusalem and the Temple, where God promised to meet with his people.

In response, the writer placed a God-sized vision before these believers. They received not only an understanding of Messiah's unparalleled, exalted character, but also a deeper awareness of the privilege they had been given to worship him and enjoy his fellowship.

God designed us to bring him glory. The opening declaration in the Westminster Shorter Catechism states it well: "Man's chief end is to glorify God and to enjoy him forever." The apostle Paul, the former Rabbi Shaul, expressed the same thought just as succinctly: "For from him and through him and to him are all things" (Romans 11:36).

The great issue in spiritual warfare is the glory of God. Satan is intent on depriving God of the glory he deserves from humanity. Unless we perceive the glory of God, our worship will be impoverished. If our worship is impoverished, we will not live with the level of personal and spiritual fulfillment to which God's glory calls us. Finally, our service to the Lord will be impeded, for where there is no dynamic worship, there is little dynamic service.

For the people of Israel, the glory of God was originally something quite visible. His majestic presence terrified them at Sinai, but was a powerful reminder that he was with them. His presence was with them at "the tent of meeting" during the many years of their wilderness pilgrimage. Generations later, when the holy ark of the covenant was taken from them, the cry, *Ichabod!* (no glory) was heard; the glory had departed from them (1 Samuel 4:21–22).

The Jerusalem Temple, with a centuries-old history of God-ordained rituals and sacrifices, was the place where the glory of God was manifested. Only a few years after this letter was written, that Temple would be burned down by the Romans after the tragic and humiliating siege of Jerusalem. It was a destruction that Yeshua had foretold: "I tell you, not one stone will be left standing on another; all will be thrown down" (Matthew 24:2).

Yet even before the Temple's destruction in 70 C.E., many children of Abraham had come to see the radiance of God's glory in a new and living way: God had revealed his unique splendor in the person of his son, "the perfect copy" of his father (1:3). To see God, one need only to behold his Messiah, the savior of mankind.

Theologian Herman Hanko speaks insightfully to the matter:

Worshippers before the coming of [Messiah] were meant to inquire into the meaning of the Temple typology as it pointed forward to him, but now believers look to [Messiah] fully revealed as the Savior who has been exalted and has entered heaven itself (see 1 Peter 1:10–12; Luke 24:26–27, 44–45). We should not pray with our faces to Jerusalem, hankering after the outward pomp of the Temple ordinances. Rather, may we be absorbed with the glory of our Redeemer's intercessory ministry in the heavenly throne room. May we pray toward heaven where [Messiah] mediates so completely for us, and where we enter by believing prayer into the holiest of all. May the worship services in our [congregations] bespeak the efficacy of [Messiah's] priestly ministry in heaven, and the immediacy of our approach to God.

It is our privilege—through faith—to dwell with Yeshua in the heavenlies (Ephesians 2:6), to sense ourselves entering heaven itself to worship with "thousands upon thousands of angels in joyful assembly" (12:22).

The foundation of the New Covenant is that Messiah, who bears the very stamp of God's nature, has come into the midst of his people. As our perception of him becomes fuller, so will our worship.

In his commentary on Hebrews, Raymond Brown challenges believers to take a fresh look at Yeshua the Messiah. "Possibly," he says, "our vision of [Messiah] is limited. We are in danger of confining him to our restricted experience or limited knowledge. We need a vision of [Messiah] with immense cosmic dimensions, a [Messiah] who transcends all our noblest thoughts about him and all our best experience of him." He is the eternal one who upholds the universe by his word of power (1:3; Colossians 1:16–17).

It is this glorious, cosmic Messiah who has brought us complete forgiveness and purification and made us forever acceptable to God, our father. The angels worship the exalted Messiah for they see in him the divine nature. Our praise is added to theirs, not only because of who he is, but also because we have come to know his salvation. We marvel that the Holy One of Israel should humble himself and die for us—that "he who knew no sin became sin that we might become the righteousness of God in him" (2 Corinthians 5:21). His greatness is revealed in his humbling himself as well as in his infinite power.

Dr. O. Palmer Robertson, teacher at an African bible college in Malawi, acknowledges that one of the most difficult things to do is to "just praise the Lord. It's much easier," he points out, "to rush into the

Lord's presence and dump all your troubles, anxieties, cares and desires into his hands than to express your wonder at his glory."

The coming of the Messiah inaugurated a new era. You and I are living in the latter part of that era, the time of a new and better covenant. Someday he who is the creator and heir of all things will return to be glorified in his people and to be marveled at by all believers. Now is the time for him to be glorified by his people who marvel at the wonders of his awesome power and unparalleled love. If our worship services are lackluster, there is a failure to appreciate the greatness of his person and all that he has done for us.

In my youth, worship was something to be endured, not enjoyed. There was a barrenness to Sabbath worship because I did not know the Lord of the Sabbath. This negative attitude is sadly obvious in many who have come to our services. The dimensions of the tragedy are worse though when those who lead in worship fail to see Messiah's presence among them. Unfortunately, at the writing of Hebrews, there were few believers able to exercise godly, informed leadership in this faith community (5:12).

Unless the leader's heart is aware of his savior's glory and presence, there will be little overflowing praise to stimulate the congregation toward impassioned worship. To encourage worship in the right direction, we need God to shine in our hearts to give us "the light of the knowledge of the glory of God in the face of Messiah" (2 Corinthians 4:6).

Bible teacher John Piper exhorts us to "see and feel the incomparable excellency of the Son of God." To that end we need to spend much time in the Word of God and seek God's help to make it personal. As God has a greater influence over our hearts and minds, so he will have a more powerful influence over our worship.

Those called to teach the Word need to give God-centered, Messiah-centered messages. The goal should be to inspire our congregations, and, in the words of John Piper, "ignite the affections with biblical truth." God is the believer's strength, song, and salvation (Isaiah 12:2). We must seek to have his spirit and truth shine through us. Worship must focus on the big themes and great truths about Yeshua the Messiah. Then the Holy Spirit will move you and your people to participate in the angels' heavenly worship, as we overhear the church proclaim in its triumph: "Worthy is the Lamb, who was slain, to receive power and wealth and wisdom and strength and honor and glory and praise" (Revelation 5:12).

We must aspire to lift our devotion to the exalted Messiah on his throne and join the hosts in heaven singing: "To him who sits on the throne and to the Lamb be praise and honor and glory and power, for ever and ever" (Revelation 5:13).

The New Covenant imparts fresh spontaneity to our worship, sparked by the presence of God. The people of Israel, for whom "the sprinkled blood" of the lamb had provided God's grace (12:24), were released from lifeless, traditional modes of worship. The terrifying mountain with its "fire, darkness, gloom, and storm" (12:18) had given way to him who speaks of his grace. "Let us worship God acceptably with reverence and awe" (12:28).

Do you, as God's servant and child, really want to worship your Lord as you ought? Dwell more on the eternal rather than the temporal. As the writer to the Hebrews instructs: "Let us fix our eyes on Yeshua" (12:2).

Hebrews 3:1 tells us to "consider him." The author uses the same word Yeshua used when he told his followers to consider the lilies of the field (Luke 12). The Lord was instructing the disciples to reflect deeply. In the same way, the writer of Hebrews wants us to reflect deeply on our savior. Spend time contemplating him, fill your heart and soul with a biblically personal knowledge of the Lord. Let that experience overflow into your praise of the one enthroned on high who "stoops down" to raise "the poor from the dust and lift the needy from the ash heap" that he might "seat them with princes" (Psalm 113:6–8), even "in the city of the living God" (12:22).

Dr. O. Palmer Robertson is right in saying,

Things happen when people praise the Lord. It's not just an idle, expendable exercise. God receives glory, people are united, truth is advanced, righteousness is proclaimed, mercy is experienced, faith is increased, and victory is secured.

All that God was ready to accomplish for a distant fellowship of Jewish believers is ready to be applied in your life as well.

CHAPTER FIFTEEN

DO NOT BE CARRIED AWAY BY ALL KINDS OF STRANGE TEACHINGS
HEBREWS 13:9

HEBREWS 13:1-19

Having made numerous references to the *Talmud*, it might be helpful to explain a little more about it. Renowned Jewish scholar, Maurice Harris, defined it as the *corpus juris* (body of law) of the Jews from about the first century B.C.E. to about the fourth century C.E. The word *Torah* (Law) in Hebrew means more than its translation may imply. The Jewish people understood their entire religion in terms of law. The first five books of the Bible are called the *Torah*, yet only part of God's revealed Law is, from a traditional Jewish perspective, contained in those Scriptures.

A theory was developed that God had revealed much more to Moses at Mount Sinai than was actually written down. These truths became part of what was termed "the oral tradition," passed on orally from generation to generation. The rabbis maintained that their sayings were of Mosaic origin. This is due in part to their intense veneration of Moses and in part to a certain understandable humility.

Not until 219 C.E. was a summary of the "oral law" compiled. When it was fully transcribed it was called the *Mishnah* (or Second Law). Much of what was later to be called the *Talmud* was anchored to this body of legal rulings.

In addition, the opinions of the rabbis were compiled into the *Gemara*, a commentary on the *Mishnah*. This, too, became a part of the *Talmud*. Many Jews accepted these writings as authoritative and used them for spiritual and practical direction. The community which first received the Letter to the Hebrews would have felt the influence of these rabbinical writings competing for their attention.

Over the course of many centuries, little has changed in the Orthodox world. They speak of *rishonim* (first ones), the medieval *Torah* scholars, and refer also to the *akharonim* (latter ones), the authorities at the time of the Renaissance and afterwards. In the sixteenth century Rabbi Yosef Caro wrote his *Shulkhan Arukh* (Prepared Table) which has become a comprehensive resource for Jews desiring a complete *Talmudic* code governing everyday life.

There are gems to be found in these collective writings of the Hebrew people. Pithy, philosophical sayings abound: "The rose grows among thorns"; "Commit a sin twice, it will seem a sin no longer"; "A single light answers as well for a hundred men as for one." There are practical elements, too: "Use thy noble vase today; tomorrow it may break"; "Attend no auctions if thou hast no money."

Yet for all of its wisdom and wit, and sometimes whimsical elements, the *Talmud* presents no distinct ethical system. Nor does it offer any coherent doctrine. What we do find is the denial of such doctrines as "original sin," "vicarious atonement," and "everlasting punishment." Human beings are portrayed as the authors of their own salvation whose spiritual life will continue to develop beyond the grave.

Who knows what strange teachings were being foisted upon these first-century believers? It is not hard to imagine that some were being urged to emphasize laws related to foods. What the issue was is somewhat unclear, but one thing was perfectly clear: what they ate or refused to eat in no way commended them to God (I Corinthians 8:8). Those who are God's children must remember that rules about food never enabled a person to establish an intimate relationship with God.

I remember when I was a young boy some of my relatives kept a kosher kitchen; they strove to follow the biblical food laws, as well as the rabbinic accretions to these laws. They did quite well. However, although they obtained "kosherhood," they did not obtain sainthood.

Our author calls us to focus upon him who is the sovereign unchanging source of our salvation (13:8). As our hearts rejoice in his accomplishments on our behalf we will continually affirm, "It is good for the heart to be strengthened by grace" (13:9).

One may begin to savor God's grace truly when he becomes conscious of the depths of his sin and his total lack of righteousness before him who is "a consuming fire" (12:29). Yeshua died "to make...people holy through his own blood" (13:12). No other sacrifice is necessary. All we can really do is gratefully offer up a sacrifice of praise for what he has done (13:15) and live a life of love (13:16).

Yet rabbinic thinking has long popularized another approach to the matter of sacrifice, particularly with respect to the concept of "vicarious atonement." According to a recurring if not pervasive rabbinic interpretation of Isaiah 53, this key messianic text sets forth the Hebrew people, themselves, as a redeeming sacrifice. The *Talmud* states that "the death of the righteous makes atonement" for others (*Leviticus Rabbah*, 20.7).

But were the people of Israel righteous? Isaiah knew that his people hardly qualified to be God's suffering servant for they were spiritually "deaf" and "blind" (Isaiah 42:19). One doesn't need to hear too many synagogue readings from the *Haftarah* (the weekly readings taken from the prophets) to see how every bit of righteousness has been stripped from us. There were more than a few Orthodox rabbis who, nonetheless, instructed those about to be executed at the Nazi death camps to see their forfeited lives as a fulfillment of the Almighty's plan to redeem a corrupt world through his people's death. Many sought the strength to embrace their death in prayer that God would use their lives redemptively. The following prayer was found attached to the garment of a dead child at Ravensbruck concentration camp:

O Lord, remember not only the men and women of good will, but also those of ill will.

But, do not remember all of the suffering they have inflicted upon us: Instead remember the fruits we have borne because of this suffering: our fellowship, our loyalty to one another, our humility, our courage, our generosity, the greatness of heart that has grown from this trouble.

When our persecutors come to be judged by you, let all of these fruits that we have borne be their forgiveness.

Stirring, even heartbreaking, the prayer and the sentiment behind it show how easy it is for people to lose their Scriptural anchor (see the admonition of 12:2). It's easy to lose sight of spiritual truths which should inform the way we seek to approach God.

Moses, himself, once offered his life as an atoning sacrifice in the place of his countrymen who had sinned; for their sakes he was willing to have his own name blotted out of God's book of life. But God would not accept Moses' life because, notwithstanding the prophet's greatness, he, like each Israelite following him, was a sinner (Exodus 32:31–33). Moses was not even able to lead Israel across the Jordan; he died at God's command on Mt. Nebo for having "broken faith" with The LORD at the waters of Meribah Kadesh (Deuteronomy 32:48–52).

But if we look back to the evening of Israel's deliverance, called *Pesakh* (passing over), we witness the establishment of an eternal principle: the blood of sacrificed spotless lambs shed and applied leads to deliverance. Those who took refuge beneath the God-ordained blood applied to their doorposts were "passed over"; their lives were spared. Passover is an eternal sign pointing to God's grace, since the Israelites enslaved in Egypt had not yet received the LORD's Law. Passover also points everlastingly to "the Lamb of God who takes away the sin of the world" (John 1:29).

We are compelled once again to consider the greatness of the person whose redemptive death is the focal point of this epistle. No one appreciated his awesomeness more than Isaiah, the chief of messianic prophets, who not only referred to him as a "Wonder of a Counselor" but also as *El Gibbor* (Mighty God) and *Avi'ad* (eternal Father) in Isaiah 9:6.

If, as the writer to the Hebrews says, we should be strengthened by grace, we need to realize that grace, if it is to be truly grace, must acknowledge God as the author and finisher of our salvation. Consistent thinking along these lines makes it imperative that God, himself, bear the full weight of our sin's punishment. And this is precisely what the Hebrew members of Messiah's body were being encouraged to believe, that God was actually and fully in Messiah reconciling the world to himself (2 Corinthians 5:19).

The people of Israel had long been champions of monotheism, proclaiming God to be *ekhad*, one (Deuteronomy 6:4). Yet the word expressing the Lord's unity was compound in character, allowing for his tri-unity. That revelation came, however, not as the result of Old Testament exegesis; it was the primary consequence of innumerable personal encounters with him in these dimensions. When you realize deep within your heart that God personally satisfied all of the demands of his justice on your behalf, inner strengthening—the strengthening of grace—truly occurs.

Spiritual survival depended on the strengthening of grace; for from the perspective of the sophisticates and self-satisfied religionists, it was the Messianic Jewish teaching that was strange, even *meshugah*. The notion concerning beasts offered on the brazen altar "whose blood was carried into the Most Holy Place" (13:11) will have raised quite a few eyebrows as the whole procedure is pictured as a typological foreshadowing of what the Messiah was to do on his execution stake.

Fulfilling Israel's sacrificial system involved bearing a curse. Not only were the slain beasts cursed with the sins confessed over them, but the flesh of the sin offering slaughtered on *Yom Kippur* was carried outside the camp to be consumed by fire (Leviticus 16:27).

Hebrews' writer sees far-reaching significance in Yeshua's suffering outside of Jerusalem's gate, "outside the camp" (13:12–13). Simply put, the Messiah died, not inside the encampment—the "holy" place—but on unsanctified ground.

Calvary was not in the ceremonially ordained territory within Jerusalem's city but upon a garbage dump whose very name had become a loose synonym for hell (*Gehinnom*). It was there, on a foul and wretched hill, that Yeshua died to sanctify—make holy—a people who would trust in him. Yeshua identified with the needs of an unholy world by offering himself in the midst of it, showing that no people need be excluded from his saving love, thereby extending God's covenant love unto all the *goyim* (nations, Isaiah 42:6).

An integral part of the *Yom Kippur* service was the confession of the people's sins over the head of a goat which was then driven into the wilderness (Leviticus 16:21–22). Translated "scapegoat" in the King James Bible, the Hebrew word *azazel* refers not so much to the goat but rather to the rocky Judean wilderness where the sin-bearing animal was banished. There's a contemporary expression which Israelis use as a euphemism for telling someone "to go to hell." "*Lekh l'azazel!*" they'll say—literally, "Go to *azazel!*"

This piece of biblical drama concerning *azazel* also finds its fulfillment in the life and death of the Messiah. At the beginning of his ministry he was driven to the wilderness—to *azazel*—and remained there forty days (the number corresponding to the number of years of Israel's wilderness wanderings). It was there that he confronted the forces of evil on behalf of his people and triumphed over sin's power for their sakes (Matthew 4:1–11). Unlike Israel, he was constant in his devotion to his father. His total obedience to the demands of the *Torah* qualified him to offer himself up "as a lamb without blemish or spot" (1 Peter 1:19), the atoning sacrifice, par excellence.

These types and images bring us back to a former observation concerning the saving work of Yeshua: it all took place far away from Israel's traditional rites and ceremonies. Yeshua suffered outside of the camp; his sacrifice was outside of the holy place. The immediate implication for the Jewish believer was clear: he could not be content to remain in his traditional setting with its outmoded, useless formulas. Perhaps there were those Jewish believers who were understandably fearful of leaving their peers, thereby incurring painful rejection. To this day, *kaddish,* the mourner's prayer, is often said by the Jewish community for people who receive Yeshua as the Messiah. In such a stressful situation believers would especially need their hearts to be strengthened by grace, grace available through "fixing their eyes on Yeshua" (12:2) and remembering he said, "Never will I leave you; never will I forsake you" (13:5). They needed to take courage from his presence, direction from his example (12:3).

Yeshua was not calling them to a life of ease; he had made it known that tribulation was an inescapable experience for his disciples (John 16:33). But in the same breath he also said that he had overcome the world and he promised sustaining grace to all who, as the writer of Hebrews says, "go forth to him outside the camp" (13:13). They could not expect to know the total sufficiency of his provisions until they turned their backs resolutely on the "obsolete" system which was slated to disappear (8:13).

No other sanctuary may be found outside of that which the believer has in Yeshua the Messiah. Everyone who would know God must leave his old ways to embrace him personally as his own incomparable savior. For the Hebrew believer this was and is especially imperative. As F. F. Bruce wrote in his *Epistle to the Hebrews* (p. 403), "What was formerly sacred was now unhallowed, because Jesus had been expelled from it," and "what was formerly unhallowed was now sacred, because Jesus was there."

CHAPTER SIXTEEN

OUR LORD YESHUA, THAT GREAT
SHEPHERD OF THE SHEEP
HEBREWS 13:20

HEBREWS 13:21–25

No image of the Messiah is more precious to the believer than that with which the Letter to the Hebrews concludes. For generations their princely shepherd's immortal psalm of comfort and encouragement which begins *YHVH Ro'i* ("The Lord is my shepherd") had ministered to the deepest needs of untold numbers of God's fearful or hurting flock.

In the *midrash* to Exodus, a story is told about Moses searching for a lost kid, a circumstance which God used to tell his temporarily disenfranchised shepherd that he will soon lead the people of Israel. That God would raise up shepherds for Israel is one thing. It was another, immeasurably more glorious thought, that God himself would actually shepherd his people.

The revelation of God's intention to do so helped sustain Ezekiel as he looked about him and saw only false prophets and feckless, self-seeking rulers. His reaction to their corruption brought stern rebuke:

Woe to the shepherds of Israel who only take care of themselves!
Should not the shepherds take care of the flock?...You have not

strengthened the weak or healed the sick or bound up the injured. You have not brought back the strays or searched for the lost. You have ruled them harshly and brutally (Ezekiel 34:2–4).

Then follows God's litany of promises:

I will rescue my flock...I myself will search for my sheep and look after them...I will tend them in a good pasture...I myself will tend my sheep and have them lie down...I will search for the lost...I will bind up the injured and strengthen the weak (Ezekiel 34:10–16).

That was then. By the first century C.E., only a vague, romanticized conception of the Old Testament shepherd remained. While the rabbis still maintained some reverence for that past image—many cherishing the hope that God would raise up a shepherd-king to deliver them from their Roman overlords—there was much disdain for shepherds in general.

Shepherding was considered a disreputable line of work. Shepherds were particularly despised on account of their flocks' habit of eating private property. It was commonplace for sheep to wander off onto another's land and consume whatever appetizing morsels could be found there. But how could a shepherd make total restitution (a requirement for acceptable Jewish repentance)? He couldn't truly repent unless he replaced everything that his sheep had eaten; but how could the shepherd know precisely the extent of the compensation required?

From a Pharisee's perspective, shepherds were among those unsavory "people of the land" who paid little attention to the Law's intricate demands. A statement from a *midrash* on Ruth indicated that it was not deemed necessary for an Israelite to go out of his way to help save a shepherd's life if, for example, the latter appeared to be drowning.

It is perhaps, then, all the more remarkable that God chose to reveal himself to the religious society's rejects, as the well-known biblical narrative informs us, "And there were shepherds living out in the fields, keeping watch over their flocks at night. An angel of the Lord appeared to them, and the glory of the Lord shone around them" (Luke 2:8–9).

Once again the ancient adage proved true: the ways of God are most definitely opposed to the ways of man (Isaiah 55:8). Paul eloquently expounded upon the concept: "God chose the foolish things of the world to shame the wise; God chose the weak things of the world to shame the strong. He chose the lowly things of this world and the despised things..." (1 Corinthians 1:27–28).

The weak and the needy are particularly the concern of the great shepherd whose sustaining and equipping love is offered in, what is for me, the most beautiful benediction in Holy Scripture:

May the God of peace, who...brought again from the dead our Lord Yeshua, that great Shepherd of the sheep, through the blood of the everlasting covenant, equip you with everything good for doing his will, and may he work in us that which is well pleasing in his sight, through Yeshua the Messiah; to whom be glory for ever and ever. Amen (13:20–21).

Certainly the Messianic Jews sensed their weakness and desperate need for the good shepherd's care. But they were not alone. Even their forebears, spiritual giants in some respects, were insufficient without his patient, prevailing care.

Francis Schaeffer, in his book *No Little People*, points out that even a quick overview of Scripture reveals the failures of those we tend to mount on pedestals. Noah was a man of faith who stood alone against the world; he also once lay drunk and naked in his tent. A careful reading of the Book of Job reveals a man who was surely not the bastion of patience suggested by James. At least twice Abraham lied about Sarah's identity; Sarah, too, lied to God saying she didn't laugh at the thought of having a child at her old age. Isaac imitated his father's lie. Jacob, the wheeler-dealer, cheated his brother. Moses not only lost his temper and killed a man but also committed an egotistical act at the rock at Meribah. His brother Aaron not only made a golden idol but then, in what must be the silliest attempt to avoid guilt in Scripture, said, "I cast in the gold, and out came this calf." Miriam arrogantly complained against God's appointed leadership. Joshua failed to purge the promised land of the polytheistic Canaanites, opening the way for spiritual compromise which contributed to Israel's undoing. Gideon routed the Midianites but then made an *ephod* which became a stumbling block to the people. Israel's liberator, Samson, remained a perpetual adolescent who never outgrew his licentiousness. David, a "man after God's own heart," was guilty of adultery and murder. His son Solomon sought and received God's wisdom but later was drawn away from the Lord by his idol-worshipping wives. Jeremiah wondered if perhaps God had deceived him; and Elijah, though an impressive figure, became thoroughly depressed after his victory against the forces of Baal.

The pattern is not confined to the Old Testament greats. The New Testament would doubtless reveal a comparable picture were its history not limited to a relatively short time span. The apostle Peter refused to eat with non-Jewish believers at Antioch and was rebuked by Paul for compromising the Gospel. Paul expressed an unforgiving spirit towards John Mark. One need only glance at the Corinthian correspondence to see acts of compromise on a much larger scale.

Although it is never stated in so many words that it is impossible to obey God's Law perfectly, even a cursory reading of the Bible reveals a people who are helpless, who cannot hope to win God's approval through their own efforts, a people who need what only heaven's shepherd can provide.

Yeshua said, "I am the good Shepherd...I lay down my life for the sheep" (John 10:14–15). The heart of the Letter to the Hebrews dwells upon the infinite value of Messiah's death for all who nakedly rely on it. But the author knows that, had it not been for the Messiah's resurrection, God's saving work would have been short-circuited. By raising Messiah from the dead, the God of *shalom* (wholeness) put his seal of approval on Yeshua's work. In fact, Yeshua's sonship was verified—even as his life's work was vindicated—by his resurrection (Romans 1:4).

Partly because of a tradition ever tending to rely on works-righteousness and partly due to the human spirit's natural tendency toward that direction, we need to join the Hebrews in being on guard, lest we ever think of ourselves as somehow deserving God's favor.

In Yeshua's parable of the lost sheep (Luke 15:3–7), the redeemed lamb's only contribution to its salvation consisted in its being found. The rabbis used to debate whether God loved more the person who never sinned (they made the false presumption that there could be such an individual) or the person who sinned but genuinely repented. Although the majority decided in favor of the former, Yeshua made it clear that there was no rejoicing over those "not needing repentance" (surely he was speaking ironically inasmuch as all ninety-nine of them were still in the wilderness).

Isaiah says, "We all like sheep have gone astray" (Isaiah 53:6). Rabbinic logic set forth *kharatah* (remorse) and *teshuvah* (repentance) as the beginning stages of a man's salvation. In the Messiah's parable, "repentance" is synonymous with "being found"—the shepherd looks for the sheep until he finds it and carries it home. So it must always be, for even the most obedient among us must ultimately confess with the Law-loving psalmist, "I have strayed like a lost sheep" (Psalm 119:176).

What does it mean to be carried home by Yeshua? Its meaning must surely be bound up with our shepherd's declaration, "I have come that they might have life more abundantly" (John 10:10).

While I was writing this book Rabbi Schneerson, whom many Brooklyn Jews believed to be the Messiah, died. Thousands filled the streets. Many were weeping. Some sat and swayed back and forth in the rain as they chanted psalms. A 15-year-old said he was hoping the rabbi would return and prove his messiahship. Another rabbi spoke for the people, "his death and burial change nothing." A 44-year-old man added, "You don't become a non-believer just because of this. He has left us with enough." True enough, from that perspective, Rabbi Schneerson left his people with a hope. Yeshua left his people with a hope, too. Yet hope is often very fragile; it can easily be shattered when its dreams go long unrealized.

Many months have now passed since the rabbi's death; there have been no rumors of his reappearance. When something has substance to it, the *Talmudic* expression used in its defense is *raglayim la-davar*, "the matter has legs." The factual basis for Yeshua's resurrection could be found in the testimony of hundreds of people who "gave legs" to the truth of his conquest over death (1 Corinthians 15:5–7). The writer wanted to see this truth indelibly engraved upon the hearts of the believers. However, he could not accomplish that if all he had to offer them was bare doctrinal assertions.

How would the historical fact of the Messiah's resurrection undergird people going through terrible *yisurim* (trials and tribulations)? Peter provided the answer when he said our father "has given us new birth into a living hope" (1 Peter 1:3). The apostle pointed once more to the Holy Spirit who activated more trust in the Messiah Yeshua, beholding his resurrection with eyes of faith, God's guarantee of victory over life's deepest struggles. The Spirit of God is also making the presence of Yeshua the Messiah real to us now.

Though not with a deep intensity at every moment of our lives, still we are, in the words of Frederick Buechner in *The Clown in the Belfry*, "shepherded by the knowledge that though all is far from right with any world you and I know anything about, all is right deep down." In other words, things are right where it really matters—between God and us. That sense of our having been reconciled to God buoys our spirits when we can find no other release from pain and perplexity.

Isaiah's consolation to God's exiled people consisted largely of this thought: "He gathers the lambs in his arms and carries them close to his heart" (Isaiah 40:11). Restoration is accompanied by intimacy, which a breached Holy of Holies has now made possible. Whatever else the good shepherd may withhold from us—good health, satisfying relationships, fulfilling work—he will never withhold himself. Because of that the believer may genuinely echo the psalmist's words, "I shall not want."

The Hebrew believers came from a tradition which spoke of God very cautiously. The tetragrammaton (the Hebrew letters *yud, hey, vav, hey*) is never pronounced. Direct references to *YHVH* occurred rarely, if ever; there was always the danger of somehow mispronouncing his name (Exodus 20:7). Expressions like *ha-Kadosh* ("the Holy One") or *ha-Shem* ("the Name") were substituted for God's name. If a Jew wanted to say "Praise God" he would say *Barukh ha-Shem* ("Praise the Name") to guard against taking the sacred Name in vain.

Yeshua told his disciples to call God *Abba*, a word which not only meant "father," but also conveyed all the intimacy possible in such a relationship. More than this, Yeshua spoke of his paternal care—the care of a great shepherd—when he said, "I know my sheep and my sheep know me" (John 10:14). The relationship he has established with his followers parallels the relationship he enjoys with his father (John 10:15). It is at a most personal level, the fulfillment of the promise previously quoted, "They will all know me" (8:11).

Rabbi Schneerson preached insistently that the age of light was imminent. Yeshua the Messiah said, "I am the light" (John 8:12). For those who trust him, that light will never fail them. Because the light is more than an ideal, but is a living person, all who are the objects of his loving care can count on his equipping them "with everything good for doing his will" (13:21).

At times we are tempted to doubt his goodness; we may question—somewhere deep within our souls—his sovereign care. But to whom shall we go? Amidst the hard realities of life we see in an anonymous medieval prayer the yearnings of our own hearts:

A stranger here, as all my fathers were
That went before, I wander to and fro;
From earth to heaven is my pilgrimage,

A tedious way for flesh and blood to go.
O Thou that art the way, pity the blind
And teach me how I may Thy dwelling find.

CONCLUSION

A PRIORITY FOR THE PEOPLE OF GOD

The world is a hostile place. Our lives are regularly confronted with difficult, stressful situations. We are bombarded by what the hymn writer called, "Fightings and fears, within, without." Because we are fallen creatures we have an innate tendency to make the worst of things. We respond poorly to crises. We often treat each other in shameful ways. Instead of helping and edifying others, we disregard them, even tearing them down. More often than not, the harm we do is an unconscious result of our self-centered pridefulness. We don't give enough thought to what the Messiah has called us to do and, more fundamentally, what he has called us to be.

The Book of Hebrews instructs us to "encourage one another." In Chapter 10:19–25, the writer calls us to focus upon the superlative way available to us to worship God intimately in the Messiah (verses 19–22), the need to persevere in the hope that is ours in Yeshua (verse 23), and the necessity of encouraging one another (verses 24–25). Without mutual encouragement our worship becomes lackluster, our perseverance difficult.

In Hebrews 3:13 we are told to encourage one another daily. Sin and hardship are powerful forces, but genuine encouragement can help us stand against their harmful impact. It is so easy to be blown off course; we can help one another to stand firm as we seek to grow together in our understanding and application of God's Word.

Before we became believers our tendency was toward hate rather than love (Titus 3:3). But our washing and rebirth by the power of the Holy Spirit changed all that (3:5). Whenever we think about the greatness of God's love for us revealed upon the cross, we should not only love Yeshua but also those for whom he died (1 John 4:10–11). Our failure to cherish the fellowship of other believers is, at heart, a failure of love. Real love, whether for the Lord or for others, cannot be expressed in a detached fashion.

John Wesley said, "The Bible knows nothing of solitary religion." You and I need one another. There were some in the community of believers who had stopped attending their meetings (10:25). They were not only depriving themselves of support (perhaps some had decided to no longer follow the savior) but also were no longer in a position where God's spirit could use them to encourage others.

Part of the work of encouragement is to "spur one another on toward love and good deeds" (10:24). The verse urges us to give consideration to that matter and consider ways to accomplish that goal. J.I. Packer is correct when he says, "We should not think of our fellowship with other believers as a spiritual luxury, an optional addition to the exercises of private devotion." God has made us in such a way that we are incomplete without others, that what stands true for the first human speaks equally well to our situation: "It is not good for the man to be alone" (Genesis 2:18).

The need for encouragement is not limited to just a few among believers. Even that spiritual giant, Paul, longed for its precious blessing (Romans 1:12). He knew that words could be the vehicle for the outpouring of God's gracious support. Because of the power invested in our speech, the apostle exhorts us all to communicate with a view to "building others up according to their needs" (Ephesians 4:29).

When I became a believer there was nothing more important to me than the encouragement I received from other believers. Although I've been a believer for more than thirty years, there is still nothing more essential for my continuance and growth as a believer.

The people of God have frequently been faced with discouragement. When the Jews were repatriated by Cyrus of Persia, many of them said, "It is futile to serve God" (Malachi 3:14). But in the midst of this depressing atmosphere the prophet stated that there were those "who feared the Lord and talked with each other" (Malachi 3:16). Their conversation centered upon their hope in God because the Lord took special note of what they were saying and "a scroll of remembrance was written in his presence" in recognition of these people whose mutually encouraging words "honored his name" (Malachi 3:16).

God listens to all we say and takes special note of both what we say and our motivation for saying it. We have the ability in our choice of words to tear down or build up. As Proverbs 18:21 says, "death and life are in the power of the tongue." The fact is that we will not always have the opportunity to offer one another encouragement. God's people are faced with the certainty of the coming of "the day" (10:25) when the only compassion available to them will be that which believers receive from their returning Lord. In that day, when we stand before him, I believe our chief regret will be that we were not a more loving, a more caring, a more supportive body of believers. As our writer said, "Keep on loving each other as brothers" (13:1).

GLOSSARY

All words defined are Hebrew unless otherwise noted.

ABBA. Father or daddy.

ALEYNU. It is our duty; the name of a prayer in which our duty to God is confessed.

ALIYAH. Go up. The honor given to the person ascending the platform to read from the *Torah;* immigration to Israel.

AM HA-ARETZ. People of the land; the common people in Israel.

AMIDAH. Standing; the name of a traditional prayer recited while standing.

ARON KODESH. Holy ark.

AVOT. Fathers; usually refers to Abraham, Isaac, and Jacob.

AVRAHAM. Abraham.

BAR or BAT MITZVAH. Son or daughter of the commandments. The ceremony by which a boy or girl at 13 or 12 is considered an adult.

B.C.E. Before the Common Era, before the birth of Yeshua the Messiah.

B'RAKHAH/B'RAKHOT. Blessing/blessings.

B'RIT. Covenant.

C.E. Common Era, beginning with the birth of Yeshua the Messiah.

DEVARIM. Deuteronomy; also, "words" or "things."

D'RASH. An exposition of a text of Scripture.

EYKHA. Lamentations.

GEMARA. The second part of the *Talmud*, compiled circa 500 C.E. Contains rabbinic comments on the *Mishnah*.

GE'ULAH. Redemption.

GOYIM. Nations other than Israel; therefore, non-Jews.

GIYUR. Conversion.

HAFTARAH. A prescribed portion from the prophets read during a service.

HALAKHAH. The way; the rules of life governing a Jew.

HASIDIM. Members of an ultra-Orthodox sect of Judaism.

HATIKVAH. The Hope; the name of Israel's national anthem.

HOSHANAH. Save, we plead.

KADDISH. A praise to God said in remembrance of a deceased loved one.

KADOSH. Holy.

KAVOD. The heaviness associated with the glory of God.

KEDUSHAH. Sanctity.

KHAVERIM. Friends, associates.

KHESED. Mercy, righteousness.

KHUPAH. The wedding canopy under which Jews marry.

KOHELET. Ecclesiastes.

KOHEN/KOHANIM. Priest/priests.

KOHEN GADOL. High Priest.

KOL NIDREY. All Vows; a prayer sung at *Yom Kippur* to ask God's forgiveness for making careless promises in the past year.

MAKHZOR. A holiday prayer book.

MASHIAKH. Anointed one, Messiah.

MELEKH. King.

MESHUGAH. Yiddish word meaning crazy.

MESHUMAD. One who is considered a traitor to Judaism.

MIDBAR. Wilderness.

MIDRASH. Commentary on texts of Scripture.

MIKVEH. An immersion in water for ceremonial cleansing, performed at various times in a person's life; the pool in which this immersion takes place.

MINYAN. Ten Jewish men that make up the quorum needed to say the traditional prayers.

MISHNAH. The first part of the *Talmud*, compiled circa 200 C.E. Contains rabbinic comments on the *Torah*.

MISHPAKHAH. Family.

MITZVAH/MITZVOT. Good deed/good deeds; law.

NEVI'IM. The prophets; one of the 3 sections of the *Tenakh*, the Old Testament.

PESAKH. Passover.

REBBE. Yiddish for *rabbi*; usually used by Orthodox Jews.

ROSH HASHANAH. Head of the Year, the Jewish New Year; refers to the holy day of the Feast of Trumpets.

RUAKH. Wind; spirit, as in *ha-Ruakh ha-Kodes*h (the Holy Spirit).

SELIKHOT. Penitential prayers asking God for forgiveness.

SHABBAT. The Sabbath Day, the seventh day of the week, when work ceases.

SHALOM. Peace, wholeness, wellness; a greeting used when meeting or departing from someone.

SHELIAKH. A sent one, an agent. Same as apostle.

SHEMOT. Exodus; also, "names."

SH'KHINAH. The manifest glory of God.

SIMKHAH. Celebration.

SIMKHAT TORAH. Joy of the Torah; the holy day when it is thought the Torah was given to Israel. A time of celebration.

SUKKOT. Feast of Booths or Tabernacles when Jews dwell in huts in remembrance of the wilderness wanderings.

TAHARAH. Purification.

TALLIT. Prayer shawl.

TALMID. Student.

TALMUD. Codified body of Jewish oral tradition; includes literary creations, legends, scriptural interpretations, comprised of the *Mishnah* and the *Gemara*.

TEFILLIN. Phylacteries; small boxes attached to leather straps which are wrapped on the upper left arm and forehead during prayer; the boxes contain Exodus 13:1–10, 11–16; Deuteronomy 6:4–9, 11:13–20.

TENAKH. Acronym—T-N-K—for the sections of the "Old" Testament. T stands for *Torah* (Pentateuch); N, for *Nevi'im* (Prophets); and K, for *Ketuvim* (Writings).

TORAH. The Law of Moses, the five books of Moses, the Pentateuch.

TZEDAKAH. Righteousness, charity.

VAYIKRA. Leviticus.

YESHIVAH/YESHIVOT. Jewish parochial school/schools.

YETZER HA-RA. Evil inclination in man.

YETZER HA-TOV. Good inclination in man.

YHVH. English letters standing for the four Hebrew letters that make up God's name: *Yud, Hey, Vav, Hey*—called the Tetragrammaton. Sometimes transliterated *Yahweh, Yahveh, Jehovah, Yehovah.* Observant Jews substitute *Adonai* (LORD) where these four letters appear in a text to avoid mispronouncing God's holy name. Sometimes *ha-Shem* (the Name) is substituted.

YOM KIPPUR. Day of Atonement.

BIBLIOGRAPHY

Brown, R. *The Message to the Hebrews*. Downers Grove: InterVarsity Press, 1982.

Bruce, F. F. *Epistle to the Hebrews*. Grand Rapids: Eerdmans, 1963.

Buechner, F. from an essay in *The Clown in the Belfry*. New York: Harper Collins, 1992.

Gilnert, L. *The Joys of Hebrew*. New York: Oxford University Press, 1992.

Hewitt, T. *Hebrews: An Introduction and Commentary*. Downers Grove: InterVarsity Press, 1960.

Hughes, P. E. *A Commetnary on the Epistle to the Hebrews*. Grand Rapids: Eerdmans, 1977.

Lewis, C. S. *Mere Christianity*. New York: Macmillan, 1960.

Manson, W. *The Epsitle to the Hebrews*. Hodder and Stoughton, 1951.

Piper, J. *Desiring God*. Portland: Multnomah Press, 1986.

Robertson, O. P. personal notes.

Schaefer, F. *No Little People*. Downers Grove: InterVarsity Press, 1974.

Sibbs, A. M. "Hebrews" in the *New Bible Commentary Revised*. Grand Rapids: Eerdmans, 1970.